Where

are

you

Mom?

"*Touched By Evil*"

Anne-Marie Mac Donald Courtemanche
Co-Author Sharon Dorival

 FriesenPress

One Printers Way
Altona, MB R0G0B0,
Canada

www.friesenpress.com

**Copyright © 2022 by
Anne-Marie Mac Donald Courtemanche**
First Edition — 2022

ISBN
978-1-5255-6814-5 (Hardcover)
978-1-5255-6815-2 (Paperback)
978-1-5255-6816-9 (eBook)

1. BIOGRAPHY & AUTOBIOGRAPHY, PERSONAL MEMOIRS

Distributed to the trade by The Ingram Book Company

Together we can do wonderful things like, help victims and survivors regain their lives that were taken from them. Thanks for your support!

Enjoy your read

Anne-Marie xxx

6 May 2022

Anne-Marie Courtemanche Camrose. July 2010

Laura Dorosh Anne-Marie Courtemanche.
Camrose Alberta 2015.

"Some people will always throw stones in your path. It depends on you what you make of them—wall or bridge? Remember, you are the architect of your life." -Evan Carmichael.

Prologue

"Abuse doesn't get better if you don't do anything—it just keeps getting worse. You must be your own friend. You must have compassion for yourself. You must forgive yourself. You deserve better. You are a precious human being and you deserve to be treated with respect. You can't ever give up. Don't hurt yourself. Hang in there—you are not alone. And it is not your fault.

Abuse often goes unreported due to cultural and familial stigma. Parents are authority figures meant to be respected not questioned.

This book contains sensitive stories about childhood sexual abuse lost love and the baby-scoop era.

This is the honest-to-goodness, true story of Anne-Marie Courtemanche.

Please, it's easy to get caught up in our emotions and in what we want, but there are others to consider and protect. Anne-Marie's intention here is to do the right thing. Her emotions are not running this show. She has decided to act right now and not procrastinate for another sixty-two years.

Remember, just because you can't see the pain doesn't mean it doesn't exist."
-Sharon Dorival

Introduction

Whenever he was drunk, or angry, which was very often; Bernie constantly called us five oldest children bastards. I couldn't comprehend why, since he was my dad. We were Mac Donald everywhere we went, until the day I happened to notice, "Sally Matthews Courtemanche" written inside of an encyclopedia. That's when it was revealed Bernie wasn't our biological father. We were given his last name Mac Donald, on the first day we moved in with him. Back in those days, it wasn't unusual to carry the stepfather's name. It simplified everything with the schools, doctors and medical insurance etc. I switched names once I completed elementary school. These first few pages are to inform those who aren't familiar with 1945 to early-1970s social and religious mores around unwed mothers in Canada and around the world. I am a product of this era which my mother was brainwashed into, called the "baby-scoop era." Sharing information about society's rules in that era, will possibly help the readers understand where my mother and I came from.

Chapter one

The following has been based on their search of Origins Canada. It details crimes against the unwed mother post–World War II.

The Baby-Scoop Era

Between 1945 and the early-1970s, in the decades after the second world war, many unwed mothers across the country were forced to give up their babies for adoption. Many were sent away to maternity homes where they were isolated from their communities. The mothers were often subjected to verbal and emotional abuse, were limited in their contact with the outside world and in many cases were never allowed to see their babies. This was called the "baby-scoop era," and it created a lifelong legacy of pain and suffering.

It is easy to forget how much of a stigma it was to get pregnant "out of wedlock" in the 1950s. Birth control pills hadn't been invented yet and abortions were illegal and very dangerous. Many women died of illegal abortions. There was so much shame and the consequences were so strong that having teen sex outside of marriage was very uncommon.

But, if you found yourself pregnant as a teenager, you often got married in those days. Some teens had shotgun weddings if they were involved in a sexual relationship. Many young women who found themselves pregnant, a common "choice" today, were pressured by their parents into "letting go" of their children, even when many of them were in love and wanted to get married so they could keep their babies.

The women disappeared from the community to hide the pregnancy, which was excused as "going to visit her aunt on the farm" or anything people would buy. But the truth of the matter was, that many of the young pregnant women were sent to "homes for unwed mothers" until they gave birth and then the baby was immediately taken from them.

The women were to return to their families and communities and expected to resume life as if the birth had never happened. The old proverb was "Time heals all wounds." It never worked. More often, the mothers whose children were taken from them under pressure from their parents grieved for these lost children as the years went by. They quietly celebrated the birthdays of their lost firstborns and forever wondered what might have been if they had been allowed to keep their babies.

In this way, the lost child has a resemblance to the lost love. Lost loves at times are driven to find each other and will reunite if parental pressure has forced them apart. Birth mothers are forever searching for their lost children if the giving up was forced on them. As the years pass it's more likely that lost loves and birth parents will search for their lost loves/child. They hope to reverse the damage to their personal history that was caused by the force of separation.

There were also teen couples in love, wanting to marry, but parents wouldn't allow it. These birth parents later reunited and married. Then they searched for their child. Sometimes the woman found the child first— located their lost loves.

In those days, when parents discovered their daughter was pregnant, often she and the baby's father were forbidden to see each other. They were told many lies to keep them apart. The girls were sent to homes for unwed mothers and forced to put their babies up for adoption. The young father many times was told she'd had an abortion.

Unmarried pregnant girls and women were considered corrupted and contaminated. In this extremely pleasant society, mostly secretively and hidden from view, the unmarried pregnant woman was seen as breaking society's law pertaining to sexuality and motherhood. The social stigma on "unwed mothers" during this period was tremendously severe. They were viewed as fallen women, hookers, whores, ladies of the evening, or femme Fatales and their children were seen as illegal, improper, unauthorized and diminished in society. These abnormal mothers were criticized and considered mentally slow or stupid, or morally incurable.

The unmarried mother could be re-established in society by keeping her pregnancy a secret, learning her lesson by giving up the baby for adoption and returning to society as a moral woman. A social expectation developed for which the unmarried mother would surrender her child for adoption. The unmarried mother was expected to simply forget about her child and change from a deviant person in society to a respectable and marriageable woman once again.

She would learn her lesson and pay her debt to society through disciplinary measures, so she wouldn't repeat her behaviour. These measures included harsh and inhumane treatment and the loss of her newborn baby. Adoption was a violent act of retribution towards a woman for not waiting to have sex through traditional marriage.

An unwed mother learned to pay the price for her criminal offence. It was repeatedly reinforced to these young women that to heal was to give up their children. This alone was a life sentence. They were unaware of their rights or of any resources that might be available. The mothers were psychologically groomed for adoption secrecy. They were left alone with little knowledge and no support for labour and delivery, making them terrified and traumatized.

All of this was designed to make it easier to get the mother to sign away her rights to her child. Restraints were used on mothers during delivery and the babies were removed while the mother was still in labour, tied and waiting for the placenta to be delivered. This created a violent trauma in the mother's subconscious, from which no mother could heal.

These mothers were denied access to their newborns and there was no such thing as eye contact between mother and baby. At times, the hospital would exchange a healthy baby for a stillborn.

Unwed mothers who gave up their babies might grieve for a lifetime. Social workers ignored that the mothers wanted to nurse their babies. Instead, they were groomed to "disconnect." The baby was referred to as "it" "the" or "that"; never "your baby." It was emphasized that the most loving thing to do was to give up your baby to a loving home. Tactics included physical threats, confinement, fear, deception and lots of covering up. The mothers might have been perfectly capable of keeping their children, as loving mothers do. But instead, they were literally forced to give up the precious little ones they had protected and carried to full-term in their young bodies. And then they were stigmatized as cold, uncaring mothers who didn't want their babies and had given them up for adoption.

A mother was released from the hospital without her child, severely traumatized, her breasts strapped, her baby taken from her along with her chance at motherhood. She was still recovering from the birth, but was warned to never tell anyone about the secret. She was reminded she would eventually forget about it, and one day have her own children. Her grief paralyzed her. She was a no-good mother who had thrown away her baby.

These unethical and immoral events happened with the approval of and the knowledge of society, which authorized these behaviours. But, these "baby-scoops" were crimes; dishonest and immoral. Unwed mother's human rights were being violated during this period.

After the early 1970s, these practices were largely discontinued. Contraceptives became easily available. There was an enormous increase in economic and educational opportunities and growing acceptance of unwed mothers, who had more options than they'd ever had before. The years between 1945 and the early-1970s with their maternity prisons, institutionalized guilt, faux-psychological explanations for single motherhood and violent, forceful adoption became a brief footnote in social history... except for the women who had survived these procedures.

These bereft mothers lived with unaddressed burdens of worry, pain and a consuming secret. The effects of the societal practices of those years are very much alive and well in the lives of millions of women.

These *"baby scoop mothers"* literally gave up their lives as mothers for others.

We must remember that in those days, religion was a powerful force and to have premarital sex was a sin. Getting pregnant was a disgrace to the entire family. You had to hurry to get married or you had to give the baby up. Women just didn't have a baby alone, unless the husband had died.

Today, adolescents have help and support. Premarital sex still isn't encouraged, but it is happening.

Files from the Children's Aid Society of the District of Sudbury

Natural Father–Hector Courtemanche
Born in Sultan, Ontario, Dec 28, 1935,

He came from a broken home where the mother deserted her eight children. He had a medical discharge from the army and received a small pension, but otherwise, the family lived on welfare and moved about constantly.

Sally stated he was very abusive with her and the children and irresponsible. He left numerous times before he finally deserted in August 1960. Sally was pregnant with John, the fifth child. Courtemanche is reputed to be an alcoholic. Further, he has been convicted on more than one occasion of assault causing bodily harm.

Mother–Sally Sybel Matthews
Born in Bathurst, New Brunswick, Sept 21, 1940,
She was born an illegitimate child and placed for adoption by her mother who couldn't care for her. She was adopted by her natural mother's sister and her husband who had no children. Sally's natural mother had two other children, both girls and both younger than her. Sally recalls her childhood as a happy time. She indicates she had a good life and they were "beautiful people. She remained with them till she married Hector Courtemanche, April 7, 1956. She attended boarding school until grade eleven at fifteen years old. She skipped grades seven and eight.

Stepfather– Bernard Mac Donald
He came from an extremely strict and close-knit family. He's been steadily employed all his life. When he began living with Sally, his marriage had just broken down. There were no children from his first union. Otherwise, he's very much like Hector Courtemanche—alcoholic and abusive. In fact, Sally pressed charges against him in 1970 for child molesting and assault and the molesting charges were never processed for some unknown reason.

This is where the CAS files on my parents and stepfather end.

Chapter two

My Story

On summer break from boarding school in New Brunswick; Sally fifteen lived with her boyfriend and his parents. This family was financially stable and well-respected in Sarnia.

Her parents were worried she'd get pregnant. Her father advised the boyfriend's parents to send Sally home; with all respect they assured him this would never happen. But, sure enough it did! Mom had brought shame and dishonour to this wealthy family. They abandoned her. She was then forced to return home. Her father told her, "You made your bed; you lie in it." Sally never heard from the baby's father or his family ever again!

A few months passed; she met Hector who was nineteen. They married approximately four months into their relationship at the Bar and Grill in Sarnia.

They moved to London Ontario where Hector was in training at the Military Base. Shortly following their relocation, Paul was born on July 18, 1956. Hector gave him his family name Courtemanche.

While in training Hector's parachute failed him. One arm was all torn up; it was essential to replace the muscle in his arm with a muscle from his leg.

The family then lived off of welfare, and a small army pension following his medical release. They moved to Espanola near Hector's immediate family.

Espanola is where I was brought into this beautiful world, on July 15, 1957. I had aspirated amniotic fluid. I remained in the hospital for nearly two months. It was vital I be pumped with penicillin. I had an allergic reaction; my tiny body was covered with giant hives. Mom later expressed how near death and how pitiful I looked.

Finally when I was discharged from the hospital; the doctor prescribed a few drops of brandy to add to my formula, to open up my appetite.

We moved around often between Sarnia, Espanola and Chapleau. Chapleau is a little town near Sultan, where Dad was born and where some family remained.

When Mom revealed to our paternal grandmother she was pregnant with Laura, she insisted Mom take a hot mustard bath to provoke a miscarriage. Mom refused!

Laura was born in Sarnia, on August 12, 1958. Immediately following Laura's birth, we moved back to Espanola.

Hector partied a lot with his friends and siblings. He'd come home intoxicated on many occasions. He'd be verbally and physically aggressive with Mom and us kids.

On one of his violent outbreaks and Mom being pregnant; he shoved her so hard into the kitchen cupboard door; it split in two.

Upon our family moving back to Espanola, Jacqueline was born, on August 2, 1959.

When he was physically present in our lives, he had no interest or interaction with us young children, or Mom. There was no emotional support from friends and family. Our lives were very unstable. This was told to us over time by relative's family, friends and is also registered in the Children Aids records.

Paul, four years old and I three, would be found going through the neighbour's trash to feed ourselves.

Nearly one year following Jacqueline's birth, Hector deserted the family for the last time, leaving Laura and Jackie ill with malnutrition.

Mom eventually met Bernard Mac Donald, who was to take us all in under his wing, feed us and put a roof over our heads. That's all she was asking for.

Laura and Jackie were so ailing it was necessary for them to be hospitalized. Laura's stomach was bloated identical to a starving child in Biafra.

Paul and I were fortunate to be spared from this disease. Proverb: "One man's trash is another man's treasure! "This is exactly what spared us from malnutrition.

Mom finally left Espanola for the last time, leaving behind her terribly miserable life. Paul was brought to Sarnia to live with Mom's parents. We other three children moved with Bernard in Copper Cliff, in the District of Sudbury.

On her separation, she was unaware of her pregnancy for John. He was born following our move to Copper Cliff on April 1, 1961.

Bernard now had total control over Mom. In that era you did as the husband requested. The man oversaw the household. Mom was a submissive woman!

Due to the lack of money, Bernard demanded Mom give up her newborn and Jackie one year old for adoption. He claimed to be unable to feed or clothe the entire family. Mom unwillingly complied, and four months later when she got pregnant with Bernie's first child, she then threatened to give it up for adoption unless she regained custody of her children. Bernie allowed them to return. Finally she gave birth to Bernie's first child, Mary in Sudbury, on July 20, 1962.

Bernie and Mom returned to get Paul. He was confused, as to whom all these children were. After all, the fifth and the sixth child hadn't been born when he'd last seen us, or even the siblings he should have remembered had changed so much as young children do in their first few years.

Under the pretense of going for a ride with this strange man, and all these other strangers they took Paul home; now to Creighton Mine. The first opportunity Paul had, he tried to return home to his dad (grandfather) and mom (grandmother). There was a search and many hours later he was found walking the railroad tracks.

He was brought back to the house; Bernie beat him. He beat him so badly it was necessary to consult a doctor the next day. The doctor confronted Mom, "This looks like child abuse."

"No, he was beaten by the children in the schoolyard." She claimed. No further questions asked.

Bernie years later explained he had no choice, but to give Paul a good licking, since he stole twenty dollars from him.

Jackie, three years old, placed a cloth on an un-shaded lamp in our bedroom; it caught on fire. The apartment now needed repairs, we temporarily moved to Mr. and Mrs. Petrucas who lived in our neighbourhood.

We soon moved into a tiny two-bedroom house, in a little town outside of Creighton Mine; Dog Patch, today known as Little Creighton. In the kid's bedroom was a bunk bed, as well as a double bed; Paul slept on the couch. I slept on the top bunk; I was awakened to an extremely loud cracking noise. The next moment I realized I was covered in ceiling tiles, saw-dust and insulation. The ceiling crashed down on me! It was a miracle I wasn't hurt.

I was terrified, in shock, crying and shaking, while Bernie was comforting me; trying to calm me down. He carried me to their bed to sleep between them. I fell asleep in his arms; at six years old.

Paul and I were a team! On our everyday half-mile walk to our one room schoolhouse it involved strolling over a beaver dam, crossing a creek and walking alongside a fairly busy main street. We also needed to pass a lake before arriving at our destination. We just loved being free with Mother Nature trying to catch frogs and snakes in the grass.

On many occasions, I'd have to go through the complete school day with cold wet feet. Nothing stopped us from being attracted to these living creatures on our little adventures. We were fortunate we didn't have any serious accidents, or anybody pick us up. Fearless and free we were! We attended this school while waiting for Our Lady of Fatima School's construction to be complete in Naughton.

We were now eight in our tiny two-bedroom house, which became very cramped. Bernie purchased a one-acre piece of property on Santala Road, in Waters Township, in the district of Greater Sudbury. Once the roof of the basement was completely covered, we moved in. We lived in this basement for three years.

There was no insulation on the bricked walls; or the ceiling. The roof was finished with plywood covered with tar paper to protect us from the snow and rain.

Wintertime was horrible! I'd roll myself into a ball on my back, while holding my legs up touching my chin trying to stay warm; rocking myself to sleep. I'd awake from being so cold; then sleep like a baby with my legs under my stomach and my bum up in the air. If my parents didn't wake up on the extreme cold nights, I'd get some warmth by cuddling a sibling.

Summertime was awful also! The windows had no screens. The cats would enter the house with mice, frogs, toads or birds to snack on. We'd have a number of bugs, mosquitoes, black flies, houseflies, spiders, mice, crickets; even the odd frog. We were thankful to have two hunting cats in the house.

The floor remained on concrete in the bedrooms. The small living room and kitchen area were covered with ripped-up linoleum.

The walls were fabricated with plywood and curtains. The cupboard doors were made of cut-up bed sheets, which were stapled to the cupboard frames.

The girl's room was next to the parent's room, separated by plywood with holes. The toilet was a twenty-litre pail sitting on the floor beneath a piece of plywood, with a toilet seat on the top. It was located on the far-right back wall with a curtain for a door. The boy's beds were closest to the curtain.

Paul at seven would have to bring the pail outdoors behind the house to empty it. When it was too full I was usually ordered to help him. If for some reason he wasn't able to do his chore, Laura and I would have to. This pail was ridiculously heavy and full at times, it would spill over as we walked. It was worse in the winter, as we'd slip on the ice, and the contents of the pail would splash on us. We would clean the spill on our clothes by rubbing some snow or ice. This spill happened numerous times, and was very unpleasant. Yet, we were never allowed to complain. I recall Laura and me using our two hands grunting and complaining to each other outside. This portable toilet lasted over three years.

There wasn't a ceiling fan, or a window to open in that tiny toilet area. The strong nasty smell was mainly present throughout the entire basement during the colder seasons. At times, when it became too intense, Mom would pour some bleach into the pail. I despised when she did that. It made the air harder to breathe; making us cough, putting us in tears and leaving an awful taste in the mouth, which is beyond words.

The oil furnace sat in the center of the furthest wall. It was mainly the older kids who would be ordered to go behind the house to fill up the container of oil. There wasn't an oil line hooked up to the furnace. Oil would at times spill on me causing much embarrassment at school.

One morning at Our Lady of Fatima, a couple of teachers and the principal, came to my class asking me to be excused for a few minutes. I was asked to open my locker, where my clothes smelled of pure oil. They told me to get Mom to wash my clothes; otherwise they would contact her themselves. I was so embarrassed. I secretly told her, so I wouldn't get punished by Bernie.

It didn't take long for the whole school to hear about this incident. Some kids would start singing, "Old Mac Donald had a farm" the moment they saw me, but this time it was directed at me. How humiliating this was. I tried my best to ignore them; not letting it show how mean and hurtful it was. Even though I was used to hearing the students sing it on our long bus ride.

During the winter months, our baths were done in the kitchen sink, each our turn for the whole family to see. During the summer months, Mom washed us outside in a square metal tub filled with cold spring water; then rinsed off with the garden hose.

The purposes for these tubs were for washing clothes with a washboard, in the good old days. Obviously, she had found another use for it, and it surely got the job done. This took place in the driveway for the whole world to see.

On a short stay at Grandpa and Grandma's in Sarnia, Bernie's second child was born on September 3, 1963 named David. We stayed until Mom was back on her feet.

We shortly returned to our home. In the girl's room were a couple of clotheslines. This one specific time Mom hung her sheets in the bedroom; while we were in our beds for the night. Jackie in the top bunk was pretending to be a ghost. The clothesline fell and she went with it, directly onto the concrete floor.

Bernie heard all of the ruckus and Jackie crying, as she tried to get up. He came in, beat her until Mom finally made him stop, which was a very rare thing. Jackie was yelling like crazy—it was obvious she was in tremendous pain. The next day she couldn't get out of bed. Mom brought her to the hospital. It was confirmed, he beat her with a broken leg. The doctor put a walking cast on her from her foot to her crotch.

Margaret was born in Sudbury, on January 30th, 1965. She was their last child together. This gave mom, who was now twenty-five a total of eight children and three miscarriages.

One night when Mom was in the hospital, Bernie entered the girl's room, picked me up and carried me to his bed. On the way to his room I questioned him, "Where are you taking me?"

"You are going to take Mommy's place," he placed me facing the plywood wall. There was a small night light in the corner of the room.

He told me to look at him, as he explained how we were going to sleep like spoons; demonstrating with his hands how they fit perfectly into one another, and then turned me on my side. He next pulled my panties down low enough to start rubbing his penis between my upper thighs, and along my external genital organs. Instantly, I began to cry. I recall my pillow being soaked! That's how many tears I spilled.

I was scared to death! I couldn't comprehend what was happening. All I knew was I didn't like this, nor did I want him to have this kind of interaction with me. At only seven, I felt it was wrong.

He told me not to cry. "Mommy does it all the time and she doesn't cry." I then cried in silence, but no one told me that silence was so loud. He eventually ejaculated between my thighs, but I honestly thought he had peed on me. He pulled my panties up; told me to go wipe myself, and get back into bed. He threatened me not to ever tell anyone, otherwise he'd go to prison, and once he'd be released he'd then kill me!

All I could do was cry and give serious thought on what had just taken place in his bed? Little did he know, Laura heard the words "We'll sleep like spoons," but at six years old she couldn't comprehend the meaning either. She wondered about it for many years.

I must say; Bernie broke me into a million pieces that night. The trauma, including the persistent sexual violations, left me with long-term emotional and psychological damage for which I had no healing for decades to come.

Chapter three

Bernie's consumption of alcohol grew progressively to the point where he drank every day, when he was home. This made things worse, because he found every reason to lash out at one of us; though he never did at his own children. I could never forget the pain and sting of the welts, felt from the belt. It was terribly difficult to sit at school on those hard wooden chairs for hours; let alone the long bus ride. But God help us, if we let the outside world know that anything out of the ordinary was going on. The most unbearable pain was from the linear blood welts left behind from the whipping behind the knees and legs. Oh, the pain! I can visualize the others getting beaten on different occasions; every beating was determined on his rage. He'd lay us over his knees, pull down our panties, and then hit us with his open hand on our bare bums. At times between the slapping he'd rub our bum. I wondered, what kind of pleasure it gave him to see us in such discomfort and agonizing pain. He beat us with a rage that came from deep within his soul. We learned to be super-vigilant, and always tried to look alert. Bernie always complained about us kids and how much we owed him. After all, we owed him our lives. Since he saved us from sure death from malnutrition? This was something that was repeated many times to us growing up. We were to show compassion for this man, as he had to endure so much? And if we didn't give him the reaction he wanted; all hell would break loose.

He never saw the candle in our hearts ready to be kindled.
He never saw the void in our souls ready to be filled.

I recall Mom sleeping a lot in those days, especially when Bernie left for work. In hindsight, I don't remember her interacting much with us at all, or even talking much. We'd be woken up at the last minute, to be rushed to dress the younger siblings, and make the lunches…eight kids in one school. Each of us ate two sandwiches. Laura and I took turns—we were the champions! We were always rushed and worried we'd never be done on time to catch the bus. On some rare days, we'd have bologna and fried egg sandwiches. Mostly they'd be just ketchup, mayonnaise, and mustard with sugar and plain margarine with sugar. The molasses sandwiches were extremely hard and dry by lunchtime. The tomato sandwiches were disgusting as the bread would be soggy. But, we learned to be happy with what we had and not to be fussy. Occasionally, we'd have an apple, or a banana; to drink there were water fountains.

Mom surrendered herself to an abusive man. She remained helpless; she could not seek support from society. Society would not support divorced or separated women and their children!

I felt for my mom.
I really felt the separation from the Beloved,
Her lost love was haunting her.
I wish I could have invited her to embrace the fire.
I wish I could tell her Bernie wasn't in love.

Back in those days, I don't recall ever seeing an electric dryer, besides at the laundry mat. We had an outside clothesline. During the winter months, Mom would wash and hang the clothes outside! It was mainly Laura and my responsibility to bring them in. We'd round up a couple of the younger siblings. We would pile up the frozen clothes onto their tiny arms, having to make many trips in and out.

This chore was exceedingly difficult, as the clothespins were frozen to the clothes; the clothes to the line. We'd frequently yank on the clothes, and then the wooden clothespins would pop off. The half pin with the spring would remain on the clothes. We'd be sure to hide them from Bernie; otherwise we'd be in trouble once again!

With the clothes still frozen stiff we would stand them on their own against the walls, or against the little furniture we had. We'd later remove the pins from the thawed clothes; we always manage to get the job done.

Once they were thawed, we'd hang them on the close line in our bedroom.

After a short while, Laura and I were taught to do the washing. We'd pull out most of the clothes at the same time out from the tub of water; putting them through the wringers, just to speed up the job. The clothes would get stuck around the rollers. The pain of my arm going through the wringer up to my elbow was terrible. I would be trying to grab onto the clothes that were stuck, without thinking to shut off the machine. The roller would then burst open! Our fingers were squashed many times. Eventually, we were more cautious. We were their mini maids! This chore was long to complete, being we were such a huge family; plus we were so young!

While being outside the kids aged three, four, five, six (me) and seven years old, we were obliged to work with Mom and Bernie. No time for leisure! Our acreage was pretty much a forest.

We were trained how to use a bucksaw, an axe, a hatchet and a scythe. Bernie would cut down the bigger trees, while Mom and we would use the axe, or the hatchet to cut the branches. Then we kids would place a couple of big branches on the ground; put the smaller ones over top, and then pulled with all our might, to a big pile to be burned. The scythe was used to cut the tall weeds and twigs.

Once the lot was cleared, the older kids needed to use the wheelbarrow filled with sand and earth to level the land.

Heaven forbid, if we tripped and dumped the load in the wheelbarrow before its dumping place. We would get a kick in the ass, a big thump on the back or a slap behind the head; as Bernie screamed at us for the whole world to hear, we were worthless and good for nothing! We were demeaned and laughed at.

I remember having so many nightmares of the devil. Today I can say I was living with Satan in disguise.

There was an awful amount of drinking going on every weekend! Thank goodness Mom never drank. Bernie was always drunk. How I dreaded the weekends! I detested getting into trouble, for the sake of the younger children doing things wrong.

Laura and I would stay on the bus many evenings during the week, so we could attend mass. We were there so often, we were asked to serve mass. We loved it! We felt useful and appreciated by many; we found great comfort there.

I really enjoyed attending church and school. Not because I was good; but to get away from the slaps, drinking, kicks, straps, being beaten for no reason, all the yelling…and a mother who didn't care.

While Bernie slaved his "arse off at work" for us; we had a bit of freedom. We had the opportunity to climb trees, make forts and igloos, play hopscotch and double-Dutch all day long. We swam in creeks with the bloodsuckers, freaking out many times whenever we found them on us. We tried to pull them off with sticks, but it wasn't that easily done. Eventually, we were informed, if we put table salt on them they'd fall off. It worked!

In our next door neighbours Aili and Arvo's back pond, we'd keep an eye on the different stages of the frog eggs developing into tadpoles, with its astonishing transformation into frogs. Was just so fascinating!

Paul and our neighbour Kevin put a snake into a jar and fed it a frog. Yes it is true, snakes swallow animal's whole. Yuck!

In my later years, I realized how blessed I was for growing up in northern Ontario; I had the chance to be closer to the various wildlife. I learned to value the many walks within the beauty of nature, and everyday living. Most importantly, it was a place to create some happiest memories.

There were few kids in our neighbourhood. There was a family of six children, who lived about half a mile down the gravel road. They had a young girl our age, who became our one and only girlfriend—Lila was gorgeous! We were grateful to have found her. She lived far, but we never hesitated to pay her a visit. We needed to keep an eye out for the black bears; but we weren't afraid. We were told to ignore them, as they were more scared of us, than us of them. Her grandparents lived next door to her.

One evening, leaving her grandparent's place to return home, Laura and I spotted two bear cubs. We tried to catch one to bring to Mom. They were so darn cute! The cubs started to run; we gave up! We told Mom about our adventure thinking she'd be excited with us, but instead in a very stern voice; "Don't you ever do that again! The mother bear is never far from her cubs. If she feels you're endangering her cubs; she'll kill you!"

Laura, Lila and I were the ones who discovered The Discovery Channel—ha-ha! Most of our exploring of our world occurred around Niemi Road and Santala Road. We loved the mountains, forests, creeks, frogs, snakes, birds and insects. Where there was life, we were there! Mother Nature is an extraordinary thing.

We lived in a Finnish neighbourhood, where everyone seemed to be related somehow to Lila. The neighbours were awesome, they adopted us eight kids, although not legally. How I wished! It might have saved us from that devil?

Lila, Laura and I would often jump in the hay barn at Eino's, Lila's uncle, before realizing the pitchforks were just lying flat at the bottom. Once we realized it, we laughed! We were fearless…as long as we were happy; having fun we were in heaven.

We'd slide off her grandparent's barn, right into the cow poop. After that we made sure our area was clear of cow feces. Lila's grandparents were never angry at us. They were very patient and insisted we call them Gram and Paappa, like Lila and her siblings did. They were more like parents to us than our own mother or father. I absolutely adored them!

Gram and I had an incredibly special connection. I honestly begged her a few times to adopt me legally…she expressed how she'd love to, except she couldn't do that to my family. I tried to convince her, I was better off with her. I could always return to my family, if it didn't pan out. Believe me I would've made it happen! I was disappointed; I sincerely thought she loved me enough to adopt me. In my head it was a simple procedure, since Jackie and John returned home following their adoption.

Grams and my birthdays were on the same day—July 15th. She would get Paappa, or her son Jack to drive us to Sudbury for the day. She always made sure I felt special, including how she spoiled me.

For my grade-four school project, she sewed a Finnish outfit. I was immensely proud wearing it. It was sewed with lots of love! I felt like a true Finnish girl—I was Gram's little girl!

We always looked forward to going blueberry picking with her, behind their seventy-five-acre piece of land. We felt protected in her presence. She explained what to do if black bears came; she was always on the lookout.

We were to put our containers down without a panic, walk away slowly, but quietly and pray they'd be distracted and eat the blueberries.

In blueberry season the bears were hungry, and no longer afraid of humans, which could be a danger for many. She was this short lady, who wasn't scared of anyone or anything—she was courageous!

She promised she'd bring me back to Finland, where she was born. Gram, unfortunately never had the occasion to return to her beloved land herself. I was heartbroken, when she passed away in August 1981; another angel gone too soon!

Laura, Lila and I were inseparable—we called ourselves, The Three Musketeers. We'd visit the bachelor men who were Lila's great uncles, whom we loved having tea, along with laughter on a regular basis. They enjoyed telling us stories of their childhood. We'd ask many questions, they were extremely patient in their answering, and enjoyed our friendly visits. They never made us feel uncomfortable in any way. NOT even when they were drinking.

There was this one married man with kids in the neighbourhood, who'd lock us up in his house. He'd try to catch us, when he did we managed to get out of the house unscathed. There were other times he'd be in his work-shed drinking and would call us in. We'd see his pants down. After witnessing that a few times; we never entered again!

Other times we wouldn't realize he was in the shed; next thing we saw him swinging his arms, as he tried grabbing us as we walked by. He'd sometimes be so intoxicated, he'd lose his balance, then stagger outside a few feet and then find his way back in. Of course, we knew he was drunk, so we never reported it to anyone. We knew in any case, nobody would've believed us.

As a result of the abuses, I failed grade two. Laura and I landed in the same grade. Like twins; attached to the hips. We'd dressed alike many times, saying we were and people believed us, more so since we were in the same grade!

When we were in grade four, Mom was diagnosed with cervical cancer, and needed major surgery.

The Children's Aid Society assigned a maid named Miss Elizabeth Cooperman. She came to cook, protect us and care for our well-being. I recall one specific time, when she cooked some smelts, which were very raw. Bernie hollered at her, as he threw his plate. He did everything for her to quit her job, but Miss Cooperman didn't budge. Nothing she could do would satisfy, or make him happy. She was devoted to us kids and she did everything to stay by our side. When she was by our side we felt secure, loved and protected. She wasn't intimidated by him at all. She confronted him about everything he said and did wrong to us. She was one courageous soul! She did her job well, and even though she didn't know it, she was our guardian angel here on Earth. Her contract was for six weeks, but Bernie had her fired after four. Mom was released two weeks earlier than planned; upon her request.

Now, my school grades have taken a beating, once again. The teacher requested to speak with Laura and me. He was concerned about us cheating on the exams. He was investigating, which one of us was copying the other. We couldn't tattle; we protected one another. The outcome was, we both failed grade four. The truth of the matter was, I was the cheater. I absolutely had no interest, or any concentration for school; my thoughts were far from my studies.

Chapter four

The slavery work outside slowed down. We slowly moved from the basement to the upstairs—into a house with unfinished walls. After a few months the electricity was connected, but the walls remained on 2 X 3 wooden studs for the longest time. Some months later; Bernie would ask; who wanted to be his helper. Paul offered, but was sadly knocked down and belittled. Bernie would waste no time stating I had more experience than him; plus he had too much homework. Oh, who knew? I was the fortunate candidate, as he'd say, except I never did offer my assistance. He thought he was the most intelligent! I knew damn well you didn't need a high school diploma to hold up wall panels. While I was holding the panel, I'd give him the panel nails, as he'd go around me. He arranged for me to remain middle; he couldn't hold back pinching, tapping my bum, or grabbing my vagina.

I was finally relieved, when I realized we had completed the walls, and the installation of the doors. But, nights never would be the same…

Bernie started visiting the girl's room, once everyone was asleep. We were five girls in our bedroom, sleeping on two bunk beds, and one single bed. Our small bedroom was off of the parent's room. Bernie knew exactly where everyone slept. So, Laura and I would occasionally get all the girls to rotate in the beds. We tried to trick him just to have a somewhat decent sleep.

I recall one night a sleeping on the top bunk; woken to my tiny body being pulled to the edge of the bed. Bernie lowered my panties enough to pull one leg out. I tried to resist by being stiff. He put his mouth on my vagina. I don't recall how long this incident lasted; I lost my thought control!

I can't comprehend how he was never exposed! He'd probably come up with a good excuse for why he was there in the first place. Mom, would've believed anything that came out of his mouth, so it seemed. She was his puppet on a string!

There were many nights when I'd have to pee; I'd wet the foot of a sister's bed. I was terrified to wake Bernie; afraid he'd come to bother me in my bed!

After, so many nights of his alcohol-scented mouth between my legs, he'd say stupid comments all of the time, like how I "smelled like piss, how I was still a little baby and that my bellybutton wasn't dry." I'd be highly disturbed by this. Thinking to myself, *well just don't put your fucking face there!* Mom, never ever said a word for him to speak better, or did she question him.

I would roll myself tightly in my blanket and slide between the mattress and the wall. Many times, I'd grab my pillow to go sleep under the bed.

To my horror one night, I woke up to Bernie's coughing in the bed across from mine. I spotted a huge bump under the blanket. I tried to cough to make noise, so he'd leave. I turned hard in the wooden bunk he made, almost bouncing in it; making squeaking sounds. After a while I just gave up and turned around to face the wall and fell asleep. I didn't want him to see me, nor did I have any recollection of him leaving the bedroom.

I never questioned any of the girls—I saved myself from being tortured. Somehow, I discovered exactly who that sister was. Laura and I never shared in detail what Bernie was doing. But, we could feel the anger, and the tension in the air, while being in his presence. At times, I'd question myself, as I had a hard-time comprehending; how and why could he do those awful things to us?

Sleeping on the bottom bunk was simple and quick—he'd crawl straight into bed under my blanket and perform oral sex on me. I wished I had the nerve to kick him, but I thought of my mother and my siblings, while keeping in the forefront of my mind the punishments that would follow.

At times, Laura and I would be doing the dishes, passing the broom, dusting, or any other chores around the house; with a smirk he'd pinch our breasts, which was very painful, physically, emotionally and mentally.

With every opportunity he found he'd pinch our bums and grab our vaginas. He constantly had his hands on our tiny bodies.

We witnessed him touching each other. Laura and I would stare at him with a look that could kill. Then we'd look at each other with hatred on our faces. It's too bad, "if looks could kill" was only a saying. Believe me he would have been six feet under many times over!

Oh, the games perverts play!
Dirty pigs!
Playing a game!
Where nobody wins!
Forbidden fruit is sweet!

As my breasts were developing, it's crazy with no exaggeration how sore and sensitive, they were. Even to this day, I've always assumed it was due from sucking them!

I finally found the courage to tell Mom about my situation. I mentioned to her how incredibly painful my breasts were. She didn't bother looking; saying everything was normal. She honestly didn't care about how I felt.

Bernie made a worktable in the basement; the top was made with a sheet of plywood. He placed it in the girl's old bedroom. He was obviously thinking ahead for his future activities—how convenient and safe this would be for him, placing it behind the plywood wall.

Once and a while, he'd pretend he was hard at work, by turning on his skill saw, drill, or pound the hammer on the table. If a younger sibling came around, he'd brush-off that little one, telling them to go find their mother. There wasn't any such luck to have an older sibling discover Bernie's activities, or for even Mom to sneak down to check on us.

It was on this table he'd turn me over face down. He'd pull down my underwear to the knees; rubbing his penis between my upper thighs, and along my outer vagina. Time after time, he would try to penetrate me, but with a couple of ouches he'd pull away. This did not stop him from ejaculating on my bum, or on my back; marking his territory by spreading the sperm all over.

My living hell continued.
My weekly nightmare!

His fucking pleasure!
Queen of Porn!
Slave of my mother's man!
Oh Lord!
What a plight.

But church was my rescue! The Church helped me keep my head out of water. The Church could rescue any willing soul, even though just for a while.

The devil could no longer frighten me with the threat of hell; my soul was already there.

How I longed for a true friend. One who would understand,
A friend that would never leave me, nor make me bow my head.
So, I ran to my favourite place to visit the lovely lady dressed in blue.
I knew she'd always understand, as I looked at her with awe
those famous silent tears would slowly roll down my face.

My blood pressure elevated, every single time I saw Bernie in those faded-out navy-blue Adidas jogging pants of his. One glimpse made me feel sick to my stomach. I knew exactly what he had in store for me.

He believed he was clever! I might've been young, but I wasn't stupid either. He never wore underwear with them. It was easier to pull them up. All he had to do to get the job done was to drop the front of his pants low enough, so should an unexpected friend pop in, or suddenly come downstairs he would compose himself fast enough, to save us both from sheer humiliation; rather than having to explain what we were doing. I was already his plaything. I didn't want to be the talk of the town too. He is certainly the most disgusting, and a disgrace to humanity!

Now, he has created a new place to carry on his next scheme, in that psychotic brain of his. I was now spared from him bothering me for oral sex, and digital penetration after I'd be gone to bed. Finally, I could try to get a decent sleep. Up to then, I'd be falling asleep in the classroom, eating, watching TV, on the bus and at times in church. There wasn't a place I could stay awake. In many ways this was truly liberating for me. No-no, I wasn't free of him! He had just created a new spot to indulge in his sinful acts.

He found just about every opportunity to have sex with me. It wasn't very hard to get me alone, since the others would vanish if the opportunity arose. Furthermore, I had a mother who seemed to detest me; she never hesitated to throw me into his arms. It was every man for him-self!

There'd be many nights we kids would lie in bed to the sound of Bernie quarreling with our mother. It would almost always escalate to the point where he'd be slapping and punching her. "You're a fucking bitch! No good for nothing cunt! You're a slut along with your fucking bastard kids." There was an instant feeling of hatred and helplessness, as I listened to those extremely hurtful words; wishing I was dead.

Come morning; after being up most of the night was extremely hard. While approaching the kitchen area, the air was filled with that unforgettable aroma, of the mixture of booze and cigarettes. The table was disgusting! The ashtrays were overflowing with ashes, cigarette butts floating in the spilled booze that were stuck onto the table; from their evening and night bash. There were plenty of empty bottles of beer and alcohol everywhere, spread out on the countertop and table.

Such a familiar sight! Again broken bottles scattered across the floor, with the alcohol combined with dried up beer. It wasn't the prettiest sight, as I walked into the tornado zone, I would visualize the damage there'd be come morning.

Listening to Mom crying, begging him to please stop screeching, bitching and cursing, fists hitting the table, slapping her over and over again; table flipped, the smashing of the thrown bottles said it all. In the bedroom we'd all be crying, we'd block our ears when things escalated and got louder.

When these incidents would intensify, Laura and I would hold the younger girls; trying to calm them down. We'd at times need to yell into their ears; squeezing and shaking them. It was essential we stifle them; we were losing control of our emotions. We definitely didn't want him to come into our room to beat us. These are some of the worse moments we had to endure.

In the morning, we'd literally tiptoes into the living room; passing the parent's room, not to wake them. We'd slowly close their squeaky bedroom door; Bernie snoring, sleeping uncovered and naked on his side.

Laura and I would make breakfast; while Paul made sure the younger kids remained quiet watching the TV. We were all cranky, impatient and argumentative due to the lack of sleep from the long stressful night. But, we managed to have everything under control, at eight Laura, me nine and Paul ten. Following breakfast, Paul would get the boys dressed. Laura and I would dress the younger girls. The younger siblings were sent outside to play; Jackie at seven, kept a close eye on them.

As I recall so well, the bastard kids Paul, Laura and I had the honours of picking up the pieces. Mom and Bernie would finally get up to continue, as if nothing ever happened. In my head it didn't finish here. These incidents will forever be embedded in my thoughts of the past!

On another cold winter evening, all hell broke loose again. Bernie physically threw Mom out of the house with neither coat, nor boots. She managed to grab the three younger kids on her way out.

He would have us all stand in a line side by side; military style. Questioning each of us, as to whether we wanted to follow Mom, or stay with him. Anyone who answered, "Go with Mom," received an extremely hard backhand slap across the side of the head, with a kick in the ass, as he threw us out of the house one by one.

He often wore his steel-toe working boots; the power behind these kicks would make my whole body elevate off the floor. I'd grab my bum with one hand falling onto the floor, trying to push myself up with the other, as best I could onto my two feet, and as fast as possible to get away. Bawling my eyes out! This is something us bastard kids had to endure. It is unbelievable, how an adult could cause so much pain and sorrow to another human-being.

When it was my turn, I wanted to save myself from the physical pain, so I agreed to stay with him; Paul did the same. Before Bernie went to bed, he nailed the doors shut, so we couldn't escape and the others couldn't get back in. When I was certain Bernie's eyes weren't on me and asleep, I snuck out of the small living room window. Paul kept watch! Once I was free, I ran for my life all the way to Grams! I slept on the lazy boy while Mom and the siblings took over Cynthia's bed and the couch.

We were kicked out of the house on countless occasions; just like dogs. Now that I mentioned it, our dogs tried to defend us when there were loud noises around it. If Bernie pounded on the table, yelled at us, or slapped us the dog would growl; bark showing its teeth. Bernie would kick it, grabbing its jaws, and squeezing them tight. He'd look into its eyes and bark back saying, he'd be a dead dog if ever he attacked, or bit him. He'd then make him lie farther away. There was nothing good about life—it was complete chaos.

Sleepovers were rare; as we needed to be sure he wasn't too intoxicated. We'd also have to judge if he was in a good mood. Heaven forbid, if something would happen to one of our friends. This was our way to maintain our silence, and protect our friends. It was not very often that we saw this guy in a good mood. It would be necessary to lie, and find different excuses, to tell a friend why they weren't allowed to sleep over.

We were mostly allowed to sleep at Lila's or Gram's on our school holidays, long-weekends, or when Bernie was gone on an overnight work trip.

The rare enjoyable times were when our parents played the guitars. This was a regular weekend event at home. Fiddle and guitar playing together, with the banjo, filled the air with their lovely voices; sang to my wounded heart.

We kids would either sit on the floor, or stand looking upwards to them. We were almost in admiration towards them. This was the harmony our souls needed. These good times were usually short lived; due to the booze!

It was an endless search to find answers. I did a bit of my own investigation. I reached out to one of Mom's dearest friends. Annie Desjardins didn't hold back expressing what a terrible mother she was. Stating she didn't deserve to have any children, and thought Mom was very selfish. On different occasions Annie would visit us on Santala Road. Saying some of us kids would go up to Mom to talk, or ask for something; she'd ignore us, and go to her room to grab her guitar and start singing. She would be in her own little bubble, as she could escape from the reality of us eight kids, who were totally dependent on her.

Annie was heart-broken; knowing she had to leave us, to endure that kind of environment. She was aware of the abuses; in the home. Claiming, she had her own problems to deal with at that time. Today she regrets not helping to save us from that living hell, and that monster. Annie clearly expressed the importance of a mother's responsibility, to always protect her children; no matter the circumstance.

I then called Sue Powell, another of Mom's friends. We chatted for a few minutes. Everything was going great. The moment I pronounced Mom's name, her tone of voice changed. She suddenly started pointing out how ill she and her husband Andy were. Also expressing how poor her memory was. I straight-out asked, if she didn't want to answer my questions, or did she honestly not remember? After a few seconds of silence; I had my answer. She implied she didn't know exactly what I was expecting from her. That was clear enough for me. I didn't want to cause any harm. I wished them good health, and told her to take care of one another. That was the end of that story!

As it's been said, it doesn't take much to amuse kids. Our fun was to challenge one another to see who was going to get the star off Bernie's bottle of whiskey. We eventually had each our turn, but this game of ours was quickly outlived. The winner had to remove it without getting caught by Bernie. The loser would have to do another sibling's chore. We all wanted to be the sheriff. We all wanted to catch the villain, and throw him in jail; there was no question who the villain was.

It was around this period in time, Bernie attempted to kill our family cat, because she had kittens. He put his foot on her, as we witnessed him putting the gun to her head: he shot her. I bawled, as I watched Tiger running for her life. She eventually came back; he finished off the job. He had shot half of her head off the first time. I wondered if cats really had nine lives, and if Tiger would come back again and again.

Bernie's nephew J.B., came from Cornwall, Ontario. He came to work in the mines in Creighton. His stay was brief. As usual, there was a great deal of drinking; loud conversations going on, as he walked into Bernie beating on Mom. J.B. furiously expressing, "You never ever touch a woman, especially in front of me!" Before we could even wink a fistfight had started on the floor right outside the girl's bedroom. We were in our beds screaming, crying and witnessing the extremely loud; yelling between them and us kids, watching each of them throw punches at one another, as we heard the blows when the fists hit the skin.

J.B. finally got on top of Bernie, shouting at us to jump over them to leave with Mom. I was terrified Bernie would grab me, while passing. J.B. screamed to hurry up—that he couldn't hold him down for much longer!

As we all were running down Santala to the Pentney's Motel at the end of the street, we heard shooting from Bernie's 12-gauge rifle. He was coming after us! Thankfully, we all made it safe and sound he never located us.

Mom took two rooms. The first night I slept in the bathtub, which was more peaceful than sleeping in my bed. We had made sleeping arrangements everywhere; some were just a blanket spread out directly on the carpet.

Mom laid molestation, and assault charges against Bernie. When I was questioned about whether Bernie had ever touched me in an inappropriate way. I responded spontaneously with a straight "No!" There wasn't any hesitation in my voice. I just said "No." WOW! New word in my vocabulary!

I was immensely nervous and shaking like a leaf, sitting in the back seat of the cruiser, in the motel parking lot. All of Bernie's threats came rushing back. I was terrified, I denied any wrongdoing of any kind and I stuck to my story.

I remember Laura going inside the police car. She didn't hesitate to reveal our secrets. She blew the whistle on Bernie. J.B. stayed a short while, until Mom recuperated somewhat.

Motel living had its advantages; we could finally breathe with ease. There was no looking over the shoulder, or walking on eggshells. I was able to arrange a stop over at my awesome friend Arlene Latendre home— she lived just behind the motel. On different occasions, I would go onto Brenda Duhamel's bus, to spend time with her; she was another bosom friend. I loved this standard of living!

As an adult, I couldn't help but wonder, perhaps I would've found the courage to break the silence; if I would've been interrogated in a different location, other than in the driveway of the motel. And maybe in a more appropriate environment, with just female constables; and without my mother sitting in the front seat, waiting for me to reveal what kind of father figure she accepted to expose her kids to.

At school, the police department had an awareness program on child molestation. They'd present short movies; followed by discussions. I was speechless! I recall tears rolling off my cheeks, and trying to hide them. It was plain to see I was shook-up; which may have indicated I had a problem? All I knew was I couldn't let the outside world know about my secrets. I was asked if I was feeling okay; as usual I answered, "Yes" End of story! Why didn't they follow up to be sure?

Laura clearly remembers, confiding to a couple of her teachers about the abuses, along with the different circumstances in our home. As usual, again we were ignored!

Mom dismissed the assault charges, and maintained the molestation charges; nevertheless nothing ever came of it. Unfortunately, our new way of life was short lived; we returned home to Bernie after a few weeks.

I guess it wasn't significant enough; Paul and I were called before a judge a few years prior. The judge questioned us; we both denied everything that was happening in the home.

I can't comprehend how adults aren't clever enough to realize how this could be so overwhelming for a young child, who is terrified to express her negative feelings about her situation. Considering the many reports of abuse, either they were playing-wise to catch the fool, who thought he was fooling them, or someone had pulled the wool over their eyes.

Mom had our parish priest, Father Delany come to discuss the abuses, which were happening in the home. Bernie made a promise to behave himself. Why make a promise, if you're innocent? He was asked to install a lock on the girl's bedroom door. Eventually, he did, except we weren't allowed to lock it.

The police asked Mom to have me examined by a gynecologist. It was reported I had genital trauma! This is something Laura remembers all so well, while hearing Mom tell her friends. Yes, but nothing happened huh?

Can you imagine how I felt as a ten-year-old child, having a stranger touching my genitals? It was like being sexually abused over again. Tears were rolling down each side of my face. I simply wanted to smother myself with the pillow. Such an embarrassing and horrifying experience for me! What was the meaning to put me through this, if nothing was to be done with the awful results?

I was left in the dark once again. How stupid! At least, if the specialist would have reported it to the authorities, the molestation charges would have finally been confirmed. Nobody could be bothered!

If this was my child, Bernie would've had to answer to me. I definitely would've done some jail time! No one in this world is to harm our children! They didn't ask to be born; they have no defense and are innocent. Protecting them is the full responsibility of the parents.

I can never forget the tremendous burning sensation, as Bernie was constantly trying to have intercourse with me. This was an obsession of his! As a result of his never-ending attempts, time after time, sure enough, it happened! Bernie RAPED me for the very first time! This time, I instantly became emotionless, my body turned numb; having no reaction, not even a tear. I believe my mind and body went into shock from the trauma. I wasn't sure what just happened, it happened so quickly. It felt like he ripped my insides out. I died on the spot! I was weak! I felt like letting my entire body collapse to the floor. I felt like a rag doll!

I was now just a hollow little girl, without any reason to live. He now was having full intercourse with me at ten. He'd pull out enough, to put some spit on his penis and then some on my vagina. I thought this was so disgusting. Only as an adult did I realized, he used his spit as a lubricant. He could now ejaculate inside of me. Oh, those uncontrollable silent tears came rushing to the surface; following the aftershock of being raped. He wiped my tears, while passing his hand through my hair. I hated everything he was doing to me. I hated him! I wished him dead many times. I often wondered, when was God going to listen to my prayers and strike him dead?

When I was eleven I went bawling to Mom. I literally thought I was dying, as I had heavy bleeding and in horrendous pain. I couldn't help myself from thinking; Bernie must've damaged my insides, or something. I wasn't prepared to tell her my thoughts!

She accompanied me to her bedroom and sat me on the bed; explained to me I was becoming a young lady and this was very normal. I screamed and expressed, I didn't want my periods, and I definitely didn't want to become a lady!

Afterward, Mom made it clear to Bernie, "You better not get her pregnant?" What on earth was she thinking? Where in hell was my mother?

He went back to his old ways. He'd ejaculate on top of my bum and back; once again I needed to clean up the mess. As the proverb says, "you just can't teach an old dog a new trick." I was his weekly grind. I soon realized I could have a break from him, while menstruating. I wore a sanitary pad the longest possible; until my skin would be, so tender and sore. He'd constantly do his touch check, by grabbing my vagina to see if I still had my periods. I figured out the cause of my many urinary tract infections.

Chapter five

Bernie and Mom managed to buy two Skidoos, on monthly payments. Family time started to be less stressful, if there was such a thing. The Skidoos allowed us to create a few family memories. They then bought a sled-like Santa's. Laura painted the two sides, with the Flintstones on them.

She found much comfort in her drawing and painting. It's just unfortunate, but certainly not surprising she wasn't encouraged to pursue her artwork. She was an excellent artist. Everyone loved her work!

With the Skidoos, we tried to focus on the more positive things. At the minimum we found some temporary fun, even though it was short-lived.

Mealtime was always filled with an incredible amount of tension. Little conversation would happen around our small homemade table, with the top finished with black and white floor tiles. It sat ten people with little room to wiggle, or move arms.

Bernie sat at the head. The whole ambience was set by him, according to his mood. If supper were a repeat of the previous day, or for some reason we forgot to do something he had asked; he would fly off the deep end, and shoot off his mouth.

He'd get to a point where you knew you couldn't run, but we also knew his patterns. The whole table would be thrown over. Whimpering in fear and afraid to make any startling moves, we would start picking up the pieces like nothing had happened, and then continue eating supper. We were scared stiff to show any emotion—after all, it would provoke him to act out in rage.

There was yet another occurrence, when he got so furious at Mom, again at the table. He grabbed the ivory-handled carving knife; forcing the blade into the skin of her wrist, threatening to cut it off. Naturally, we started to cry. He shouted at us. "And if those fucking kids don't stop crying I'll cut it off!"

We looked at Mom in silence, as she was crying from terror, not sure if he'd actually cut it off. We weren't in any position to take that chance. Tears rolled down our faces, while we were trembling and doing our best to stifle ourselves, so the pig wouldn't hurt our mom.

Eventually, he released her. She made a dash for it, heading straight for the front door. The carving knife followed!

Bernie looked at us; slammed his fists on the table, as he stood up and yelled, "I am God!" You know at some point we had no other reason to think differently. Since we had no proof of another God it was hard to believe that he wasn't. The fear he had instilled in us could be tasted. He was in control and in his eyes; we were just bastards and good for nothing. Always repeating how we'd never amount to anything good.

We had a family friend, Mr. Locke. He was a distant neighbour, who lived at the end of Niemi Road which was off Santala. He asked, if we older girls including Jackie and Lila might be interested in making a few dollars; cleaning his home occasionally. It was an instant Yes—any excuse to get out of our sick home environment and Lila joined our team.

There were times we'd need to walk that mile and a half to get there; he always brought us home safe and sound after our hard day's work. We were nine, ten and eleven. I can't imagine what that house looked like, once he let us paint his entire house!

Mr. Locke came to visit Bernie, they were drinking. I overheard their conversation. You couldn't miss it, they were very vocal. I was standing a few feet away in the living room. They argued in the kitchen. The rooms were separated with wall paneling. They were negotiating on a price; Bernie was selling me to Mr. Locke, as if he were selling a piece of meat, or something!

They agreed on one thousand dollars; I was terrified! I went to Mom in horror, crying my heart out. She pulled away saying, "Don't be so silly." That's all of the support and comfort I was able to squeeze out of her.

Though the selling never took place; this goes to show you the control Bernie had over us, and how he put us through endless anxiety.

We carried on cleaning his house regularly. He was another great bachelor; at no time did he ever try to make any advancement on us girls. Although, I recall mentioning to the others, we should never under any circumstances be alone with him; especially since he accepted the deal from Bernie. I had my guards up!

Even though the whole ordeal was Bernie's idea! It was normal for me to doubt Mr. Locke was waiting to have sex with me too. My thoughts horrified me; knowing he could actually do the same sexual acts Bernie's been doing for years! We girls agreed, and promised we'd stick by each other and stayed alert.

Over time we felt secure in his presence; able to laugh and finally have some fun. He honestly was a genuinely respectful man.

Those day's air-conditioners were a rare thing. On those extremely hot days, we'd put on our bathing suits and go for a swim in the pond, located on his property; with the frogs, water lilies and let's not forget those water spiders!

Celebrations

I could never celebrate my birthday alone. Paul's was on the 18th, Mary's on the 20th and mine on the 15th of July. There was one cake for the three of us.

I don't recall getting many gifts from my Mom. My favourite was when she would wrap quarters, dimes and nickels in pieces of waxed paper, and then place them between the two layers of cake; before icing it. This was what made my birthday celebrations special.

Some years depending on the atmosphere in the home; we were allowed to invite one friend each for lunch. Since our birthdays were during the summer holidays; Lila was our guest of honour.

But most of all, I looked forward to celebrating with Gram. She was the one who always made me feel incredibly special. Again I wasn't alone, but when it came to her, I would've done anything to please her. She was one of the few amazingly lovable people I knew. I've always felt her unconditional love, as she went out on a limb to please me, especially on our special day. I was her special Annikki!

Thanksgiving

Thanksgiving is a graceful celebration, as we demonstrate our appreciation and gratitude for everything we have. In class the teacher would ask the students; what we were thankful for. I'd have no choice, but to lie.

We said grace before our daily meals. Thanking God for being alive, even though I was internally dying. I frequently prayed for him to come to save me and get us out of this horrifying place called home?

Holiday's just gave him an extra chance and opportunity to drink more and more. For many, Thanksgiving was just another national paid holiday, free from work and school. Bernie added dread to every holiday. Thanksgiving wasn't anything special in our home!

Christmas

Christmas was a complete different story. I tried to open my heart to believe in the magic and miracles of Christmas! I loved decorating the freshly cut Christmas tree, Paul and John would cut and drag out of the bush. Visualizing like it was yesterday; making popcorn strings with the siblings and Mom; singing Christmas carols, laughing and having fun. These are a few precious memories I hold dear in my heart.

People doing things for one another out of love, hope and remaining optimistic, as they share good cheer, reconnecting with families and friends to bask in the good times.

At school, it would've been nice to join in with everyone's excitement about Christmas, but at the forefront of my mind, was the reality that awaited me at home. There were no joyous Christmas tunes to lighten my spirit. We were blessed that Mom always managed to put together a wonderful Christmas feast; even though we'd have to pick our meals up from the floor.

I remember receiving groceries, including turkeys, toys and clothes that were delivered to the house sent from an association in Sudbury. We were excited and appreciative of all donations.

Christmas Day was my biggest nightmare of all. Bernie would drink from morning to night. He'd get up still drunk from Christmas Eve, continue drinking and go back to bed. Only to get up again to perfume the air with his cigarette smoke; drink even more whiskey, scotch, wine and beer. You name it, he had it on display.

There was no limit to his drinking, or his violent outbreaks. We'd have to walk on eggshells and try to keep our distance, which was scarce as gold, as those old people would say. We didn't want to trigger anything. His rage on this special day was very upsetting, frightening and lonesome.

There was no one to talk to; no one to help. I made up songs for the broken-hearted, but I didn't dare sing them out loud. This house was the Heartbreak Hotel. Many people knew what was happening; nobody could be bothered. We were doomed to fall through the cracks. We were royally screwed!

I couldn't even compare myself to the other kids. I grew up feeling ashamed, guilty and empty. I was one frightened child, left to her lonesome in an unsafe world, without even the confidence to battle a worm. Where was the love that I longed for? Where was my mother to stand up for me?

Every girl deserves a father who will guide and protect her. Oh Lord, look where things went wrong. The Virgin Mary wasn't listening to the pleas of the unlovable and lost daughter, who belonged to no one in particular. I wondered what I was living for. There was nothing to stir me positively from the inside out. We were always in survival mode—always waiting for hell to break loose!

Most memories of my childhood are intertwined with alcohol and sex somehow. I couldn't even sing, "I feel good." He kept me crying. Nor could I twist and shout. I was broken badly. There was no R.E.S.P.E.C.T.

This was not what I needed. There was no mama to take me home on no country road. We were not united and nothing was making any sense. The radio brought me no solace. It only heightened the disturbance taking place in my mind. I was indeed on the Highway to Hell.

I just had to put up with it; accept my wretched life. Every year it was the same. Nothing much ever changed; except for the violence outbreaks, and the excessive drinking intensified.

I was taught Christmas was a peaceful time. It was a special time to celebrate with love; they forgot to mention Christmas wasn't meant for my family. Christmas didn't exist at our place. Christmas never came to us. Santa didn't know our address.

Bernie obtained himself a good secure job as a truck driver, working for Loeb IGA. He'd sometimes be gone for two nights straight out of the week; which was very nice. He mentioned to Mom how he'd like to take Laura and me on a truck trip to Toronto, in the transport.

We agreed only because we assumed we'd be going together. When the time came we learned we were to be taken separately. Now, there was no way in hell Laura and I wanted to go anymore; Mom insisted we go!

Laura went first, and on her return, all I can remember was her saying; she'd never go on another trip with him ever again. Her anger and disappointment were expressed by her facial expressions; as she made eye contact with me. I knew she was furious, her mouth closed tight, as she rolled her eyes they said it all!

Only as an adult did she tell me, she was so terrified she peed herself!

My turn! I literally went crying to Mom; the best she could say, "You wanted to go—you go." End of that discussion!

He stopped twice going to Toronto and twice coming back; stating he needed to rest, it was dark but he lied! It was for me to give him oral sex each time, with the help of his hand on my head. When he was at his sexual climax, he would push my head up off of him and ejaculate in his hand. I can assure you it was the longest, most dreadful and last trip I ever took with him.

Our parents purchased a tent trailer, a boat and motor. I can't express how exciting I was to finally get away from the everyday living hell home environment.

Believe me, these were no regular camping grounds. Before entering the parents were obliged to give a count of how many people and animals were to enter the forest. On our departure, a worker at the gate would verify our presence.

We'd drive for miles on this logging road, which was operated by a lumber company, in the city of Massy. This road travelled northwards into the Canadian Shield, as it snakes along parallel with the River aux Sables, going even further into the wilderness.

There were many man-made roadside assistant pits for the truckers. We'd camp at these pits, mainly where water was easy to get to access. We'd fish, swim, use the water for cooking and washing the dishes; life was good!

We'd fall asleep to the sounds of the wilderness. Most importantly, it was very peaceful and liberating, but freedom always comes at a cost!

We'd occasionally have a two-minute visit from a forest ranger, checking to see if everyone was safe and sound. It was an amazingly secure feeling, since we were the only human around sometimes for days.

When we'd go to bed, Bernie had the last say on where we'd sleep. The three boys slept on foam mattresses in the pickup.

This particular evening, he told me to sleep at the foot of his bed. I didn't think anything of it; we were many sleeping next to one another. I woke up to him yanking on my blanket with his feet. I tightened the blanket and fell back asleep. Once again, he woke me with his foot in-between my legs; suddenly I let out ouch! Which surprised me! Loud enough for him to finally stop; he scratched me with his toenails.

While in the forest, he figured he'd teach me how to drive. I wanted to take someone with us. He obviously had this planned out with answers to everything; saying everyone else was going to play, or they had chores to do. Again one on one! I did find it odd, but not at all surprising; he didn't offer to teach Paul. He took me leaving everyone at the campsite, including of course my mother. She never ceased sending me with him; no matter his demands. I gave her a look with my mouth closed tightly; I'd be shaking my head *noooo*, yet she didn't pay attention to the signals I was sending her way.

Once again I was reminded, I had nobody to protect me, or speak up on my behalf. I was endlessly hoping Mom would magically snap out of her heartless ways; rescue me from the limitless torments.

Bernie would insist I sit close to him, almost on top of him with wee space between us. He'd put his seat back then pull me closer; he could put his arm around me to grab one breast; the other in my panties.

He would press the gas and brake pedals, while I grabbed the steering wheel. I almost drove off of the road a few times. I lost sight and my thought control! On a couple of occasions, he had to break instantly. He'd park the pick-up in a pit; lower his pants enough for me to hold his penis, putting his hand over mine to help him ejaculate. We return to camp, as if nothing ever happened. I would bring myself down by the water to try to find some peace of mind; trying to put my thoughts in order.

This driving education, thankfully, took place just a few times. I honestly didn't want him to teach me how to drive. But, I knew deep down that "no" wasn't in my vocabulary. Mom, would've arranged for me to go in any case. I was around eleven or twelve years old; with not even a thought of obtaining a driver's license.

Back at the house, he would tell me to put a blanket over him; while lying on the couch, as I'd be told to sit at his feet. Over my pajamas, he'd wiggle his toes on my vagina. I felt like screaming! The thought of me giving him a karate chop on his legs crossed my mind. As usual, it was just a thought!

I was a lantern that didn't shine. I had lost my talk. Bernie took my talk away. He took my talk away leaving me only with thoughts—thoughts that were killing me slowly, because I could not let them out.

Many times I'd sit on the floor, caressing myself and feeling my emptiness. He'd waste his breath calling to me, but I simply pretended that I couldn't hear him. Mom would then tell me to go to him to rub his feet.

Oh, Mother! What did you know?
Your little girl is no longer a virgin.
Wake up, Mom!
Mom! Where are you?

Did she not know? Or was she just turning a blind eye to my plight? Why was she always pushing me on him?

Chapter six

I survived this corrupt chaotic life, now to the age of thirteen; still playing a role that wasn't mine. Mom was hired at the IGA in Creighton Mines—she was the assistant butcher; a couple of days a week. Things in the house would drastically get out of control with us eight kids; with a lot of bickering. When Bernie was home he'd often send the other's out to play before supper, locking the door behind them; or sending me to do it. I would hear the kids asking him, "Why doesn't Anne-Marie come out?"

He'd reply, "She is going to make supper!"

I'd begin putting supper together; he'd then call me to his room. I felt like screaming my lungs out! I didn't want to, thinking to myself *when the hell will he leave me alone?*

Now, with mom at work we'd have intercourse on their bed. Things were now moving on to something new. Another time, with the kids locked outside; he asked me to bring him a cup of tea.

When I entered the bedroom, he was lying in bed; his legs spread apart with just the corner of the blanket covering his genitals. I placed the cup on the night table, as I turned to leave; he insisted I sit for a moment.

I did! He wasted no time removing his blanket. I was in total shock! This was the very first time seeing his complete genitals. I couldn't believe my eyes!

He took my hand, placed it on his baseball-size testicle; his over mine. This was the moment he revealed he had only one testicle. He claimed to have had an accident, while climbing a fence as a child. He released my hand; I didn't waste a second, pulling mine off of his genitals.

I went to escape; he grabbed my wrist saying, "Sit down I wasn't finished." He told me to hold his penis and kiss it. I fucking didn't want to do that; I wanted to die right there and then. I froze and couldn't move or say a peep!

He pulled me closer, so it was easier for him to put one hand on my head, holding his penis with the other, forcing my head down on him; instructing me to put his cock in my mouth. I resisted; I fucking couldn't do it! With his penis going down my throat, I was choking and coughing, I just about vomited. It's too bad I didn't vomit all over him. I was pulling my head upwards; he'd only push down harder. Selfish bastard! He ejaculated and told me to swallow it. I did! I just wanted this to end and get the shit out of my mouth. How fucking disgusting!

As far as I recall, the previous time I perform oral sex on him was on the trip to Toronto, a few years prior. At least then, he'd ejaculate in his hand.

He remained in bed; ordered me to continue making supper. I was still in shock! I literally went to the bathroom, brushed my teeth, sat on the toilet and bawled my eyes out, with my face between my knees.

I would put myself together, with the best I could; carried on as if nothing happened. I put on my imaginary mask and went on completing the supper. I wasn't very talkative that evening. I needed time to comprehend what had happened on that bed. Other times he'd tell me to go spit it out in the toilet. It's just too bad I didn't bite the fucking thing off; only in my thoughts!

Laura and I were doing the dishes this one particular evening; Bernie walked by saying, "Anne-Marie come downstairs and help me."

Laura knew what kind of help he wanted. She couldn't hold back her words; "I know what you are doing to Anne-Marie." This girl had some nerve!

OMG! Bernie turned around in a rage, started chasing her. It seemed like she might run out of luck only by a hair. I swear to God he was just one strand of hair behind her. He was swinging his arms trying to catch hold of her. I was petrified! I can't even imagine how my poor sister felt? I knew if he caught her, she'd be dead for sure. I thought *don't worry sis. One day we will rise and we will bring him down! I didn't know how, but this abusive father will one day be exposed.*

It was her lucky day, and she got away!

Bernie went downstairs, I followed. This incident surly didn't prevent him from his sexual obsessions. He continued as if nothing happened. This incident was never discussed.

Oh yes! Now, for something funny! Laura and I caught a turtle in the nearby creek. Laura called Mom at work to see if we could keep it, God bless our lucky stars she said, "Yes." Bernie wasn't there to influence anything. Mom said, "Put it in a jar."

Laura said," it's too big and we certainly don't have a jar big enough to hold it." Mom, "find a pail." Laura, "It's too big!" Finally, Mom said, "Put it in the square metal tub we use to bathe outside in."

We tried! Laura called back explaining it still didn't fit. Mom couldn't imagine what kind of turtle we had caught!

It remained in the square tub; it was lopsided. When Mom got home she was stunned! We had caught a giant snapping turtle! I would pay a fortune to have a picture of her face when she saw it!

She expressed how fortunate we were; the turtle could have chopped one of our hands, or arms off. The following day, she contacted Laurentian University in Sudbury. They were extremely interested; they brought it back to the university. They were astonished to see exactly what kind of creature we had captured. They mentioned it had probably escaped from its freshwaters. Laura and I felt honoured; we were two proud little Heroes, donating to science.

The homes were at a distance from one another, between Gram's and ours were four houses and some open fields; with a little area between Gram's and Emil Basto's house that was solid bush. This is where we had seen bears come through many times. We once again saw two black bear cubs.

We decided to slowly follow them. We were always attracted to these beautiful round balls of black fur, which roamed around us so freely. We weren't giving up! We absolutely wanted to prove to Mom it wasn't impossible to catch one for her. She would always comment on how beautiful and free they were. We tried, but we were never that lucky! Or were we?! We had totally forgotten her warning words from the last time we'd told her. Again, she instantly lashed out at us repeating, "*Don't you ever go near a bear cub!* You girls don't listen!

After this incident, Laura and I learned to just admire them at a distance. We'd make noise, so they'd stay away from us. Our school bus at times had to stop to allow the mother and her cubs to cross in front of the bus.

I must admit we were brave and adventurous little kids. John and Paul would walk to their judo class in Lively; just over one mile away. We were walking machines, walking everywhere!

Bernie would insist they fight one another, to demonstrate what they had learned. He took great pleasure in seeing Paul humiliated in the presence of all the siblings. Bernie would have us pair off and fight one another. He especially enjoyed pairing one of the two boys with one of the girls. Like Paul and me. If the girl won, as I did once; the degradation of that boy would commence?

Bernie would literally push the boy around, calling him a suck, faggot and engage in a battle with him, saying he'd never be able to beat his old man, "Not even when you're a grown man; I'll always be stronger than you!" To be in his presence was torture!

I realize how frustrated and angry I must have been. Having it all bottled up, and taking it out on Paul. I remember just letting myself go wild, having no self-control and not knowing what I was doing. I used Paul as a punching bag! Funny to say the boys were taught to never lay a hand on a girl. Paul probably backed off, or he'd be punished for fighting me. For that kindness, his reward was mental punishment by Bernie, who had a thrill of damaging the boys psychologically.

Laura and I were enrolled for sewing class. We had no choice, but to walk the darkness of the night, since we lived out in the boonies; with no streetlights. Batteries were scarce for our small flashlight, so you bet, at times it was spooky! We absolutely appreciated seeing the moonlight especially on those foggy evenings; we'd scare the heebie-jeebies out of each other.

As we all know, kids have extraordinary imaginations. With the different noises coming out of the bushes, hearing the wolves howling and the cracking of the trees; we made it home surprisingly early at times. But this wasn't something we'd let win over us. We continued being our fearless young selves. If we had each other, we could conquer the world!

We'd knock and ring at the police station to bum a ride home; we hit it lucky many times. They'd ask, "Why are you girls wandering around so late. Don't you know how dangerous it is to be roaming the streets at this time?" We were always so grateful for getting a lift. There were the odd times, they didn't respond. We'd ring and ring and ring, and if there'd be no response we had no other option, but to carry on our way. We'd leave disappointed and exhausted from our long day!

Once the sewing class was terminated, we signed up to join Brownies and then Girl Guides. We'd leave following our supper as dusk was falling; we'd be singing, clapping our hands and whistling just to make noise to frighten the wild animals.

Now, Jackie joined us, we became a threesome! The walk to Waters Township School was about a mile and a half away. These programs helped us regain our self-esteem and confidence; just to have Bernie crush us over and over again.

Another memory Laura and I have is being burned by Bernie on our arms or hands with hot spoons, instantly taken out of a cup of coffee, or tea, a lit match instantly blown out; also with the tip of his cigarette. This would take place as we sat at mealtime. We'd usually react with ouch pulling our arms away; laugh to show him it didn't hurt, but damn, it did! He'd do this to seize our attention—we were to concentrate on our food, no dozing off—no talking, unless we were addressed by one of the parents. If we were to cry or complain we'd be belittled, or even dismissed from the table.

We were dragged by the ears, so hard they would crack. I swear, I'd be holding onto my head as he pulled on it; seriously thinking he'd pull it right off.

Another joyful time, of course Bernie went to work, we decided to build stilts with the lumber that seemed to be just lying around. Paul cut and nailed the blocks, to place our feet on. We had a blast until he returned and realized what we had done with his lumber. He snapped, ordering the five bastard kids to kneel in the kitchen.

We were demanded to kneel with our backs straight, facing the wall; until we delivered the name of the person who had made the stilts. He pointed out where each was to kneel. The furnace vent was engraved on my knees; it was tremendously painful and deep; due to the length of time kneeling.

We threatened poor Jackie to say it was her; otherwise we'd all beat her. Naturally, she confessed. The issue was, she was the fourth eldest child. Bernie said, "She definitely didn't do it alone!" We were all sent to our bedrooms. Before he entered, we'd hear the snapping sounds from the folded belt, as he pulled at each end. He would whip us each our turn. All you could hear was *"Daddy! Stop! Daddy! Stop!"* over and over again each our turn. I'd be squirming in hopes he'd miss my body on a few swings! Putting my hands behind, to minimize the back and bum pain; only to have them whipped too. He stopped only when he decided we were in enough pain.

Not once did Mom ask him to stop the beatings.

One time, Mom got up from her lazy boy chair, and I sat on it; on her return she ordered, "Give me my chair?" I answered, "Sit on the floor frog where you belong!"

She started to swear and gave me her evil look; with one eyebrow higher than the other. When she did that, it meant serious business. I jumped off fast, and ran outside to the end of the driveway; turned around, she was standing in the middle of the driveway. I hollered at her, "you're too fat to catch me!"

I couldn't believe I had just spoken to my mother like that! I was always the incredibly quiet little girl who kept to herself. Guess I was pushed to my limits of her not defending, protecting me, or anyone else for that matter. At the same time, I suppose I was being a smart ass because she was French. A French frog!

Mom said, "You need to come in at some time; you wait and see. She had to throw in; "Just wait till your father gets home," something she had the habit of doing. Of course we'd beg her not to tell, since we were punished many times for no reason. He enjoyed inflicting extreme corporal punishment on us. We certainly didn't want to inspire him, or give him any reason to go crazy.

That was Mom's strategy to get out of taking responsibility for being a mother and it surely worked for her—she didn't even have to lift a finger.

What a reliable and affectionate mother she was! I have no idea what planet she was from; I was sure she wasn't from the same one I came from.

Mom never touched us physically. The most she did was shouting and swearing a lot. When I came back she sent me to my room for the night.

I once mention how I was fed up with living there, and I wanted to run away from home. She simply said, Go, nobody's holding you back! I did just that, leaving right after supper; I didn't want to sleep on an empty stomach. I started to walk, pretending I was literally running away. I didn't see, or hear anyone call my name; nobody could be bothered! I spent the night with Chuck in the doghouse. Next morning on my return, we carried on as if I never left; no questions asked.

When playing at Lila's, and we felt the need to extend our visit we'd call home; we were told to be home at a certain time. If we forgot to check the time, we'd be sent to bed for the night without eating.

Whenever we realized we had passed our given time; even by five minutes, Gram would give us something to eat. She was aware we wouldn't eat until the next morning. This woman was our savior! There were many evenings we'd go to bed on an empty stomach—not even a snack.

Since I'm on the topic of food! We were forced to eat the fat, the skin, along with the many forgotten prickly hairs on the pig's feet. Another tasty meal was stew—Bernie was cooking up this pot of Irish stew that smelled out of this world. I can still visualize him standing at the stove. I suddenly saw him spit into the pot. He laughed, saying he'd mistaken the pot for his spittoon; he didn't bother spooning out the chewing tobacco, as he continued stirring. Whenever there was a new meal; house rule was to compliment the cook, expressing how delicious it was.

It was a long time coming, but we finally got running water, and plumbing hooked up. Laura and I were responsible for washing the younger kids.

One evening Laura and I noticed John's neck was filthy! It was black, either because we didn't wash him properly, or from passing the full day outdoors, playing in the sand. Once and only this one time did I come up with a great idea—I grabbed the floor brush to wash his neck, it was necessary for it become clean. Poor guy was crying, while I was scrubbing him. He was red with little bumps in the skin caused by the bristles on the brush. Let me tell you he was cleaned! But we'd get in trouble, if ever we didn't do our job right. Bernie did his inspection after seeing John's neck. You can be sure we were vigilant when cleaning the kids from that day forward.

The parents and the three boys were lucky; they had the privilege of going on a trip to Red Rock-Northwest, Ontario to visit Grandpa. We five girls envied them, but we soon realized we were the fortunate ones. We were free from Bernie!

We had the best babysitter ever Sheila Husson. I must share this with you. I joined a group on social media; I noticed the same name she had. I wrote and asked, if she babysat the Mac Donald kids on Santala Rd? Sure enough it was her! We were both surprised that we've reconnected after over fifty years.

Sheila shared how she clearly remembers, chasing after the rabbits with us, every time they escaped their enclosure, which was about every three to four days. She will never forget the cat having her kittens in Jackie's bed.

The scariest moments were waking up to hear the black bears grunting and scraping the exterior unfinished wall of the girl's bedroom. They were trying to get to the rabbit pelts that were hanging to dry.

Sheila agreed to watch the five girls for one week. That week passed with no news from Mom, or anyone. Her parents along with herself started to worry, thinking of the worst-case scenario. About four days past the date they were supposed to return. Sheila finally received a brief phone call from Mom, telling her they were not ready to come home. That's pretty well how that phone call went! Mom didn't give a reason, date, or even a clue to when they would return home. That was the only call she received from Mom. They just simply didn't come back for two full weeks. I must say, I wasn't surprised when she mentioned how the pay didn't reflect what it should have.

How we were amazed at how a twelve-year-old could accomplish everything she did!

I was relieved when I saw her response to my question, stating Bernie never touched her. The only thing she had to say was, when in his presents; she had bad vibes.

We did raise rabbits to eat and sell. At one point we had over 200. The rabbits would chew on the chicken wire and free themselves. Then we all went into a frenzy trying to catch them. Our miniature poodle Lady Bear rounded them up for us. Fun times! Then when the rabbits fattened up, it was time to make a killing. There were no alternatives, as we were taught how to kill, skin and gut them.

With one strong whack with a solid wooden club, Bernie would hit the rabbit behind the ears; hung it by one leg on a tree branch. Using the sharpest hunting knife possible, he'd slit open its throat to let it bleed.

When it stopped bleeding he'd cut down around the two legs in-between the legs and pull the fur down around its head. He'd afterwards slice its abdomen to empty the guts. There was one rabbit that Bernie hung and slit its throat; squealing extremely loud, kicking and trying to free itself. Poor thing wasn't dead. Bernie beat it, but it didn't want to learn how to die. Bernie agreed, if I didn't care to continue doing this awful job.

This one time Paul was running an errand, he realized our family dog Sam had followed him. He yelled at him; threw rocks to scare him enough to return home.

This had worked previous times; not this time! He was struck by a station wagon. The man who hit him was kind enough to bring Paul back to the house; he announced the terrible accident, as he apologized to the family. He was very saddened by this!

Bernie ordered Paul to go back to beat the poor thing's head, with a rock until he died. We all cried, Paul cried too, but having no free will, Paul obeyed Bernie's orders like always. He put an end to Sam's suffering. How cruel can a person be to get an eleven or twelve-year-old child to do this to his pet?

Mom read books pretty well every night, in Bernie's absence; when he left on a night trip for Loeb's. When the clock would ring in the morning, she'd many times shut it off, or just let it unwind until it stopped on its own. It was an alarm clock that needed cranking.

She'd remain in bed, dozing off and on; she'd shout at us older kids to hurry to get the little ones dressed. One went on to do the lunches, while the other dressed the kids. Often we didn't have time to make breakfast for the younger ones, nor for ourselves for that matter. The morning's Mom did get up; she'd help us make breakfast.

When we'd be running late for the bus, we'd make a sign to the driver, one minute. The driver was very patient, but when it was impossible; we'd give her a signal to continue on her way. It was unbelievable how often we missed the bus. There were times in order to catch it, I'd throw a sweater over my pajama top to hide it—how humiliating! Other times I'd jump into my runners without socks. We'd leave for school, many times on an empty stomach.

The school was three miles away. When we missed the bus, we'd generally stop at Gram's; she'd ask her husband to drive us to school. They spoke Finnish, which made no sense to us. Next thing we knew, Gram said, "Have a nice day," and then off we went with Paappa. Of course, there were the odd times he didn't want to take us. She'd then turn around to ask her son Jack; at times he'd be kind enough to say, get in the car without being asked. But of course, there were the rare times it was necessary to walk. We'd make it to school for lunchtime. We'd take our time walking on the railway tracks, and the busy highway; we'd make signals to the truckers to blow their horns.

One day, Laura and I hitchhiked to school. A truck driver stopped, Laura and I hopped up; we didn't feel any danger. Thank goodness he was a nice man, who dropped us off at our school. This was an isolated incident. When Laura and I were together we often felt invincible.

We deeply appreciated their rides in the winter; Even though a minus forty degrees back in those days occurred more often than today; we didn't let that bother us. We'd put on extra clothing. We'd be sure not to miss the bus coming back. Laura and I many times remained on the bus, to attend the 5:00 o'clock mass, in Lively!

This reminds me, for a short period of time; Bernie drove a school bus for the Protestant school board. I often wondered if he ever molested any other children.

We seldom had the permission to leave the yard on a school evening, with the exception of attending church, or other activities we signed ourselves up for. I was exceptionally pleased, on this one beautiful evening Mom sent me to play baseball, with my classmates down at the end of the road. I even had the privilege of getting off of doing the dishes. Baseball was one of my favourite sports. We played till the minimum brightness of the night set in.

Chapter seven

As I approached home, I had my three brothers, David six, John ten and Paul fifteen crying hysterically in the driveway. They had a hard time catching their breath; they were hyperventilating. I finally understood what they were trying to say; "Mom was gone and left us!" She left with the four girls, and had no idea where they were headed.

I raced into the house to see for myself! Panicking, and running into every room; sure enough everyone's clothes were gone. I must say there was one hell of a mess! We needed to clean it up; it was apparent they needed to make a fast exit. I couldn't believe a mother could do that to her children; why the hell didn't she take me?

There was no indication she was planning her final exit. I never saw her pack a single thing, nor did she ever hint she was leaving.

I, too, was in a state of shock. In Bernie's absence, I would many times beg Mom to move out; insisting I was fed up with the beatings, fighting and drinking. I never did admit I was being sexually abused; it was no secret to her, she was already aware! I had no courage to take control of my life.

Never in my wildest dreams did I imagine she'd leave us behind. I thought, *Holy shit!* This just confirmed to what extent she really hated me. She'd really outdone herself this time, by abandoning me to prove it. Wow! I realized right on the spot, hate is a deep feeling. It had grown in Mom maybe because she felt neglected, mistreated, or abused. But, why turn against me? What was her reason for allowing hate for me to well up within her?

Oh, Mother! Hate doesn't heal. I hated this life just as much as she did! Lord, where was justice? I was devastated and I knew exactly what was in store for me now. Heaven forbid!

Things had fallen apart, and I was left to put everything back together. How could I cope with this shock? How would I survive? But, I refused to become what I feared. I became a child of steel, hard as a rock with no tender feel. Once again, my past had won.

I attended to the boys, we wept in each other's arms; until we had no tears left. John and David followed me everywhere—the situation was a total disaster, with many broken hearts. I reassured them —that I'd take care of them and wouldn't let anything happen to them.

On Bernie's return, he saw how devastated we were. He was incredibly angry too; apparently he also had no idea either. But, I had the impression, he was mostly angry at Mom for taking his Martin guitar!

He comforted us by saying; he'd do everything he could to make us happy. He warned us not to talk to our siblings at school, or we'd be in trouble.

Growing up he'd threaten us, saying he knew people everywhere, if ever he found it necessary to find something out. The only thing left to do was continue to believe him.

Laura approached me, and wanted to speak to me at school. I told her I wasn't allowed, and walked away. This was extremely painful and heart-wrenching, but at the same time I was angry she'd left me behind, which made it so much easier for me not to communicate with her. John spat in Laura's face when she approached him on the school ground.

My whole life was demolished again. I'd gone from being a fourteen-year-old adolescent, who loved baseball, to becoming an instant full-time mother of three boys, a maid, their cook, their teacher, their protector and Bernie's "wife." This was the most catastrophic thing my mother could have ever done to me. While I was mothering my brothers, and at Bernie's service; Mom was finally free. My worst nightmares continued, and were now escalating. There were no limits, no specific time, as to when Bernie would do whatever he desired. I couldn't comprehend anything; my emotions went numb.

Over the years of abusing me, I gave him different signs, expressing the pain and discomfort I was experiencing; every time we'd have sex. He never gave a damn. "Me myself and I," that's exactly who he was.

Now I became his property at fourteen, he wasted no time insulting me; expressing, how he too was in discomfort and it hurt him as well, when we had sexual intercourse. He'd constantly mouth off saying; I was drier than a bone when having any kind of penetration. So, to have intercourse he continued to use his saliva, as a vaginal lubricant. Penetration was very painful. It felt like my body was experiencing electrical shocks every single time. I felt like puking!

I wanted to run, but there was nowhere to turn. I was in prison and paying my dues.

The memories continue to haunt me today and I beg *Dear God please let my torments be the cure that another woman needs.*

Laura was mothering the sisters, as Mom would leave with guys. She was responsible for ensuring the sibling's homework was complete, everyone ate; most of all she cared for their safety. Mom partied a lot once she walked out on us. She was a man-hungry woman on the loose. She dated many men, brought them home and slept with them. Laura would be sleeping right next to her bed. Little did Mom know, Laura was waking up to the sounds of them making out?

Chapter eight

My saving grace, at this time was beyond the shadow of a doubt. I'd finally found my sweetheart, my true love! He was Lila's oldest brother Dave. I shared my very first affectionate kiss with him. I was always thinking about him!

As far as I can remember, he's always been around; as far back to when I was six years old. He was a friend and Lila's oldest brother. As he grew older, he started different projects at his grandparent's place; he was around more. Gram and Paappa were very present in their grandchildren's lives. Paappa helped Dave and his younger brother Tom in building a canoe, along with a motorized flying airplane; it was impressive seeing it fly!

Dave was a busybody, who enjoyed working on motorcycles and Skidoos in Paappa's basement. When it was time for harvesting, the guys baled hay. They'd place the bales on the huge trailer behind Paappa's tractor. I loved my window view, watching them work in the fields. I would feel the intense need to daydream, while having the desire to be truly loved!

Gram would let me know when Paappa's brother, William his wife and the girls, Heather and Vicky would come for a visit from Sudbury, making sure I'd be present; feeling like I was part of the family. I've always felt I belonged!

I started to find Dave extremely attractive. This wasn't a baby crush! My female hormones were acting up on me. I'd have butterflies whenever I saw, or spoke to him.

He'd start up conversations more freely. He had a terrific regard, leaving me with a smile every time! Moving his eyebrows up and down, as he'd wink at me. When he was near me, he'd pass his hand down my spine, giving me goosebumps! He had long dark-brown hair, golden-brown eyes and measured five-foot nine. I fit to perfection under his arm. Everything was just so perfect, especially together in each other's arms. He'd walk me home many evenings.

He was sixteen and I was fourteen. He gave me a new reason for living; emotions I just couldn't and didn't want to live without. I realized he was interested in me; soon we were head over heels in love!

Our best meeting spot was at Gram's. We'd go downstairs to be alone; I'd watch him work on his different projects. Whenever he was too occupied and needed extra concentration, he'd bring me home. I found it extremely hard to be separated from him.

He'd ride close to my house on his chopper; I'd sneak out to meet him. How I loved that feeling of freedom with my arms around his body; holding him tight.

Naturally, we saw each other secretly; I wasn't allowed to date. The few people aware of our love affair were Gram, Paappa and Helen. We were together everywhere and every chance we had. We'd be intimate in the open fields, under the stars, under the moonlight, in Gram's steam-bath and downstairs at Gram's. Let's just say, as two people in love; anywhere was a good place!

Let me tell you, a little story Dave reminded me of. He was to sleepover! Things started to escalate; our passion was growing stronger by the minute. I made him tea; put on a baby doll nightgown. As Dave put it; I changed into something more comfortable. Bernie was to be gone on an overnight trip.

Suddenly, we heard his truck pull into the driveway. There was no back door to run, so we started to panic. Dave immediately dove under the bed. I recommended he remain there until I gave him a sign, when the coast was clear. Thank God, he jammed himself up against the wall, Bernie did look under the bed; he was just too overweight, to be able to bend all the way down. He questioned Dave's shoes, my response was delivered with no hesitation; Helen gave them to Paul.

He returned home once it was safe. We both were irritated at Bernie's unexpected return; at the same time, relieved we didn't get caught.

He had been frightened for his life and rightfully so, after hearing the many awful stories.

This incident didn't stop us from being together. Dave played music in the high school band. I'd sometimes meet him there; we'd have a few dances between performances. When the evening was over we'd leave together on his motorcycle.

Wow! At fourteen, I had unwillingly replaced Mom after she abandoned me, to enjoy her glory days. I did everything a wife was expected in a home. Although, I had already accumulated plenty of experiences in many different areas! Whenever Bernie felt the desire; I was at his service. I was my stepfather's sex toy; there was nothing I could do about it. He'd try to make me have a digital orgasm; I'd squirm saying it hurt; he'd stop and continue having intercourse.

At this very moment, I'm having a flashback of him in the missionary position, doing his thing. Out of nowhere, I would ask if we could go shopping; to buy a dress for example.

He'd tell me to shut up and stop talking; he expected me to enjoy him making love to me. In my head I was vomiting. I knew what making love was—this had nothing to do with love. This was abuse! But he didn't care; he never stopped.

He couldn't hear my thoughts anyway; I knew nothing of what happened on the bed; allowing my thoughts to fade into the far more pleasant art of lovemaking. Dave and I had mastered it! As I grew older, what we had created lingered in my mind, as beautiful memories.

Let me say Bernie was totally annoyed with me, when I wouldn't pretend to enjoy myself. My feelings were hurt; naturally I turned my head and cried. I wasn't asking about a new dress to bug him. My best explanation for that was; I absolutely had no interest in what he was doing, it seemed like I was numbed by his actions. I was thinking like a typical teenager with shopping on my mind; having a slight difference of interest!

I did learn to shut up, to keep certain calmness in the home. I caught on; the job would get done faster. It appeared, I had what I wanted, and although it was rare I asked for anything in particular. I can absolutely say he bought my silence.

I'd be facing the wall; the tears would soak the pillow time after time.

He'd turn my head to kiss me, putting his tongue practically down my throat. He'd stop and say, "You're not dead! Put your tongue in my mouth!"

Unwillingly I complied, so disgusting! He'd then tell me to move mine around his; I couldn't, I froze stiff. I would feel his warm saliva run down my throat. He didn't even know how to kiss, I was gagging!

I was obviously, his sex slave! Even when he woke up at 2 a.m. or 3 a.m. to leave for work, we'd sleep together until the alarm clock rang. I'd quickly jump out of bed; like a newlywed, never without a smile, to make his coffee and breakfast. As I did, I was wishing his death—that gourmet breakfast was missing the rat poison. I prayed he'd have a deadly collision.

As an adult Paul shared his perceptive; he became delusional and blamed me for Bernie abuses towards me. Indicating, I was always in his bedroom. I made it clear; he definitely should have defended me, instead of turning a blind eye, him too.

I reassured him; there was absolutely no pleasure of any kind; thoughts of such cruelty sickened me. I was angry that he could even imagine that! I was always threatened by Bernie; like him and the rest of the family.

I was learning how the world operated. The abused become the accused when they are older. They are judged by what they have done in the past. Everyone makes mistakes in life, and though it took me some time to learn from mine. I knew damn well I had never signed up for this! No fucking way I asked for it! Dad abused us all, just in different ways!

The tears I shed were because of fear. The kicks that I took, my brother deafened my ears. My sister forced myself to become immune to the blows. The pain faded yes, but my mind grew weak. As my body grew fuller, Bernie was mesmerized by it, so I became his freak. He said he'd teach me, but when I was no longer afraid I wanted to die.

Paul expressed we should be grateful; he put a roof over our heads and fed us.

I said, "What! I paid a fucking price!"

To help us kids recuperate from our grieving and sorrows, Dad did what he thought worked best, buy-buy-buy! He bought us a new 50cc dirt bike and himself a new 500cc Kawasaki motorcycle; within a few months, he bought a brand new 350cc Honda Gold wing for Paul. We were back to having a few pleasant times.

Paul received a ticket for turning on a red light, in Sudbury. When Bernie discovered this, he turned over the bike to me. Paul hated me for this; it wasn't my fault—it was Bernie who controlled every move we made. I was on the wild side with the bike in my hands.

I rode it everywhere. I rode full speed down Santala Road; on the gravel. I had a slight rebellious streak against my parents and furthermore against the world. I was lucky I didn't kill someone or myself. I'd drive on the highways—nothing could stop me. At only fourteen and definitely no driver's license!

As winter was just around the corner, Bernie bought me a snow-jet. He had a Skidoo and Paul had inherited Mom's. We did our best with these toys, to create some good times, and try to cheer everyone up.

I would ride on Dave's motorcycle and Skidoo every chance I had. Our love continued to grow stronger every day until I became pregnant. I didn't know it, but I had really bad morning sickness; I literally thought I had the flu, little did I know!

Bernie would tease me saying, "You're pregnant," he'd laugh. At the same time he'd throw in "I hope it's not Koski's kid."

I contemplated on how to break the news to Dave. There aren't many ways to announce serious matters like this. I arranged to meet him at Gram's; broke the news there. I pronounce those words, I'm pregnant, and his first reaction was, "Let's get married!"

I told him it wasn't the best reason to get married. I explained, my mother was married and pregnant; been through hell, and that's not the kind of life I envisioned for myself. Deep down in my heart, I knew if he would've persuaded me just that tiny bit more; things might've turned out differently. From the very first day we'd started dating, I imagined spending the rest of my life with him. I absolutely adored him! He was the best thing that ever happened to me!

We sobbed in each other's arms for the longest time. I thought to myself, after having the baby, if ever he still wanted to get married; I would've said yes!

Whenever Bernie would tease me about my pregnancy, my reaction was "ha ha!" But, it was mind-blowing; to even think I could be pregnant; after a few months, I realized it was true.

I don't know how or where I found the strength and courage, but it was essential I leave the boys, especially Bernie!

I started communicating with Laura at school, implying I wanted to move in with them. I finally left home when I was nearly four months pregnant. It was devastating, having to separate myself from my brothers; they were so dependent on me. It was now Paul's chance to finally get on Bernie's good side.

This was extremely difficult and heart wrenching for us all. Our family was to be torn apart, one more time. I had no other alternative, but to leave my heart behind on Santala Road!

Chapter nine

Arriving in Creighton; I woke up to cramps in my feet and legs. My mother didn't waste any time saying, "You are pregnant with Bernie's baby!" I snapped back, "No! It's Dave's!"

I was furious. *I thought you bitch! You left me behind knowing I could get pregnant by him.*

She said with a smirk! Dave and I were lucky, he was a few months short of eighteen when I got pregnant; otherwise she would've laid statutory rape charges against him.

I remember, cutting her short from her senseless lecture, which she was pretending she cared. I didn't waste a second more, swearing and yelling in anger. "Are you fucking crazy? You don't know anything about me. I love Dave and nobody will ever stop me from loving him." Now, I was worked up, pissed off and becoming hysterical. I had my index finger in her face, screaming at her, "You knew exactly what Bernie was doing and you abandoned me; you left me there! You're fucking sick in the head and I'll always hate you for that."

Of course, she ended that conversation pretty fast. Next day, I was brought to the medical clinic. Sure enough, "pregnant!"

She said, as she cried, "You did just like me, pregnant at fifteen!"

The doctor explained how lucky I was; too far along to have an abortion. I lost my self-control and snapped; expressing how he could never have forced me, into having an abortion.

A short amount of time passed; we moved to Sudbury with Mom's new boyfriend.

He was eleven years older than me; fourteen years younger than her. Well now, it does seem like history was going to repeat itself. Naturally,

I was having a hard time accepting everything that was happening to me and around me. I quit school, and isolated myself from the outside world.

Mom started doing exactly what she did with Bernie—pushing me towards her man. She made me feel so ashamed yet, sent me for walks practically every evening with Richard Williams. He was the only one who would listen to me at the time; he tried to make me feel important again. At least going for walks was a way of releasing some anxiety, and getting away from the noisy bootlegger's beneath us. What a bad choice for our first apartment, once leaving Creighton Mines.

Though, not very responsible for a mother of five young girls! She didn't hold back on expressing how embarrassed she was to be seen with me in public; I too should be ashamed. It hit me! Once again, I was reminded how much she hated me! She was ashamed, ashamed of herself, or ashamed of me? Sad to say, we had very little in common; we couldn't stand each other.

I was perplexed about seeking answers that didn't exist—holding on to a hope that my mother couldn't give. So naturally, I didn't want to see anyone. She also made me feel dirty like a good-for-nothing piece of shit.

I had been searching for the love of a parent, since I can remember. I felt like a stranger, I clung to Mom, but she was a stranger to me and to herself. Where did I belong? Home! That's where I longed to be. But, what did home look like? How could one describe home, when hell was all they'd been through?

I tried to persuade her to take walks and she'd say, "maybe tomorrow, another night, or I'm tired," even though she didn't work. Otherwise, she'd start to swear, so eventually I gave up. I yearned for a mother's touch, and the compassion that a good hug can offer.

She played guitar and sang downstairs at the bar—if we wanted something, we knew where to find her. I didn't ask for anything! I never thought she was playing for me, nor was she? Mom and Richard spent more time downstairs drinking than with her kids. The worst days were — Friday and Saturday they'd come up between 4 a.m. and 6 a.m.

Before this, I hadn't really seen her drink. She was very loud and rude! She'd say, "You don't need me to talk with. I'm sure you're ok without me." My perception of her was that she used us children, as if we were her servants, she'd always be sitting on her chair; asking for this and that; go buy me Pepsi, cigarettes chips etc.

After many evening walks, Richard declared his love to me! I had no reaction; his words went in one ear and came out the other.

We continued our walks. We started discussing my situation; he'd express how I'd make an awesome mother. Also how he'd support and respect any decisions I made. He promised not to reveal to Mom what was developing between us, and I could have a hundred-percent trust in him.

We walked farther than our usual spot, I insisted we stop. I was getting tired and cold. He gave me a nice big hug. A hug was something I deeply needed. Dave was the best hugger; was it because it was true love? His arms were the only arms I ever felt secure and safe in.

Next evening's walk; he repeated he loved me, which was accompanied with a hug and a kiss. I didn't know exactly how to react, since he was genuinely nice; full of compliments. But, he was my mother's common-law husband. I had to be an adult, and put an end to this right there and then!

We went back to the apartment. I stayed out of sight for the next few days. In hope, if I was invisible and stayed in my room his feelings would perhaps vanish. Let's not forget I was fifteen; him twenty-six.

Mom called me into her room—where she spent her days and evenings, reading and watching TV when she was home. She asked, "What's wrong with you? You seem pretty quiet these last couple of days."

I thought to myself, *oh what do you care?* But instead, I replied, "Oh nothing. I'm just listening to the radio and reading."

She said, "Why don't you go for a walk with Richard? It will do you some good, since it's been a few days since you left the apartment." We then returned for our walks!

He was such a sweet talker. I felt desperate and needed someone to converse with; also someone who would acknowledge me as a person. I was pregnant, lost and very alone. I needed someone to hear, and guide me. Fear was my constant companion, and silence was my loudest cry. I feared not knowing what was going to happen to me with my pregnancy.

Mom decided to get involved in my life; by getting a social worker from Children's Aid to come into the home, to discuss my pregnancy. This woman sent a nurse to give me prenatal lessons; I learned how to deliver naturally. It was a good opportunity to learn about what to expect during pregnancy, childbirth and at the beginning of parenthood. Except, at a young age having a lot of anxiety, could make you forget things you've learned. I was taught about the baby's development, preterm labour, relaxation techniques; variations in labour, breastfeeding and infant safety, amongst other topics. She never prepared me for the true realities.

About a week later, the social worker returned, this time to take me to Kitchener-Waterloo Ontario; a home for unwed pregnant girls. As it turned out, she and Mom had made arrangements to have me sent away. I freaked out! I had no choice; at only fifteen, this was just another bomb-shell of Mom's. I felt like a dog, someone had dropped off and wished me good luck.

I'd call home to speak to Mom, but after only a few minutes, she'd pass the phone to Richard since we never had anything important to say. He'd tell me he missed me, which my own mother could never say to me. Sadly, but honestly, I missed our walks and his kind words he'd express so freely to me.

I was allowed to reverse the phone charges back home once a month. I was this lost soul, at the other end of the world, in a strange city, with no family, no friends and nobody who cared. The ones who did weren't aware of my situation.

Back in the days, long distance was awfully expensive; Mom didn't have a penny to spend on me. Gram and I would speak often over the phone, and never did she complain. We'd even send each other letters; she'd sometimes surprise me with a five, or ten-dollar bill. She was always there for me.

In recent conversations with Dave, he told me how he didn't have any news about me during that period of time, but was always hopeful. I'm assuming Gram and Helen thought it was in his best interest to not give him any information that involved me—he was taking my leave very hard. They were probably hoping he'd forget me, and eventually move on. He was put to shame, and had to live with the guilt that he had brought dis-grace to his whole family. It's just today I believe their intention came from being brainwashed into the beliefs of the baby-scoop era!

I carried my baby with love and affection, talking to her and rubbing my baby bump every moment I had. I remember the wonderful sensation of being pregnant, telling her she conceived with love. A love that was very special! In my heart of hearts she was Dave's end of the story! But, there was this little voice telling me, there was still a tiny possibility it could be Bernie's. I did my best to blur out those negative thoughts and feelings.

With the help of a social worker from the home, I began to put my wall down, slowly and began to interact with a couple of girls. This took every part of me to open up slightly; which was satisfactory to me. Otherwise, I remained in my bubble, with my thoughts. In this home for unwed mothers, no one judged anyone. Everyone accepted and took responsibility for what was happening to them. We encouraged each other in a positive way; let's not forget the respect for each other's personal choices.

We were tutored for school. There was necessary aid, psychologists and social workers, if needed, or if one of the responsible workers thought someone did. Over a short conversation, Mom mentioned I should look up the Courtemanche in the phone book; they were my uncles. Visiting was uncomfortable and awkward at the beginning. They welcomed me with open arms. At least this got me out of the home for a few hours once and awhile.

I was at this unwed home for nearly five months. One early afternoon, I was interrupted, and heard my name being called over the intercom, asking me to go to the front desk. I was dumbfounded, to see Bernie standing at the front door! I instantly felt my blood pressure rise, but I was used to hiding my feelings. We sat in the parlor, next to the office for a short visit. He then mentioned, John and David were waiting in the vehicle and he needed to leave.

That's all of the conversation I remember, or even if he ever came back. John as an adult recalled going to a place in Kitchener; they were ordered to stay in the vehicle. This is when he learned Bernie had come to visit me—he hadn't told the boys what he was doing, or who he was visiting! How we would've loved to see each other.

As for my first childbirth experience, it wasn't very exciting, nor was it pleasant. I had an epidural, so when it was time to push, I couldn't feel my contractions. The nurse kept repeating, "Push! Push! "

I snapped! "That's what I am doing!" But, obviously I wasn't pushing hard enough.

The nurse was literally on top of me, with her arm over my baby bump, forcing the baby downwards. Out came the baby! I gave birth on July 29, 1973 to a beautiful girl weighing 6 1/2 lbs; named Christine Lynn.

I had just turned sixteen two weeks prior. The nurse presented her to me for a few seconds, as she remained in her arms. I wasn't allowed to have her on me. She was taken from me, at that very moment! I was stitched up and brought to my room.

I was heartbroken; I couldn't even hold my baby for two minutes; after waiting nine months to see her and to have her in my arms. The nurse completely refused my parental rights, at this time. After a while I couldn't restrain myself; I felt a tremendous emptiness and I insisted on seeing my baby! The nurse was kind enough to show me through the glass window.

I was hurt and confused; this apparently was the closest I could get to her. I gave the nurse an attitude, expressing, she was my baby and they weren't allowed to keep her from me! The nurse replied, if I continued they wouldn't even show her through the window anymore. I calmed down in hopes of eventually holding her. Which didn't happen?

To speed up the healing process of my stitches, the nurse placed a heated lamp under a blanket, between my legs. To ease some of the pain, I was given a rubber inflatable cushion to sit on.

This was all so surreal, as if I was stuck in one never-ending nightmare. I must say I felt humiliated and disrespected by certain staff members; feeling like they judged me because of my age! It was traumatizing, and one of the most horrifying events of my life.

There are so many memories I have forgotten—some good and some not so good, which could be a great thing in my situation. Many happy memories from those days have escaped from my mind.

I had visualized the day I'd give birth, then holding my baby in my arms. Isn't that what every mother looks forward to while being pregnant? But, those few real beautiful visions were quickly washed away. It was difficult to see through the fogginess to find the missing hours, due to the overwhelming amount of stress that exceeded my ability to adapt.

I returned to the girl's unwed home, a few days following my delivery. My tears were endless! I spent one-night there; I packed up my personal belongings.

But, most of all I was missing the most precious thing, my baby! I may not remember the songs I sang in my hurting heart to her, hoping it would reach her soul, but I adored her. And as much as they denied me, I knew she belonged to me!

I wasn't allowed to take her with me. I was told there had been arrangements made, once again by Mom, to pick her up following my arrival in Sudbury. I was shipped off on the Greyhound bus. I sat at the back all the way to Sudbury. I didn't want to see, or speak to anybody. Sitting on my stitches, I felt every possible little bump on the road. I cried for the longest time; before falling asleep, 286 miles away from home. It was a peculiar feeling, I felt like I was moving from the brightest to the darkest cavern.

I even once thought, Mom was trying to get back at Bernie, for not loving her as promised. It also crossed my mind that she would take revenge on him, by sending me away impregnated with a child she thought was his.

I wasn't given the chance to say, "Hello baby I hope you enjoyed the drive? Welcome to Planet Earth. Hope you enjoy your stay. I know our journey was a little difficult, a little painful, perhaps even a bit fucked up, but regardless welcome! Life fades just as quickly, as it is brought to fruition, so please treasure the time you have!

There will be moments you wish would never fade, but they will fade, but never let them escape your memory, and seek to make more of those moments every day. Never stop dreaming—soon you will realize that life is the most difficult journey you will ever go on. But, life can prove that the journey can be rewarding as well. I wish you the best of luck, young dreamer, but never allow your dreams to become your master."

Chapter ten

While I was away, Mom, Richard and my sisters moved into a nearby rental house. On my return, we soon returned to our daily walks. I was awfully lonely, not to mention how confused I had become. Mourning the loss of everyone and everything I'd ever owned and loved, I felt tremendously hollow, the emptiness had control over me—I was now incapable of having love.

I disconnected from the world, and didn't give a shit about anything anymore. So yes, Richard and I had a sexual relationship, which was short lived.

Then eventually, there was a false wedding that occurred between him and Mom. Again, we were all disgusted and confused by this; we were clueless to the planning of their wedding. Everything was done secretly with her. As young teenagers, we were not at all as stupid, as she thought we were!

We found it unacceptable that they could just come home to announce their marriage; not even one of her girls was aware of it. We were furious! We felt betrayed and ridiculed! It was the neighbour Mary, who spilled her guts, saying the marriage was a sham. She knew firsthand, as she and her husband played the roles of the two witnesses.

We never knew which foot to dance on. I was fed up with the constant lies and drama. I finally moved out, and never looked back. I found a room and board downtown; I stayed for a few weeks. I didn't feel safe or comfortable sharing the same kitchen with complete strangers.

Later, I stayed at the YWCA for a short period. Here it was essential to register at a certain time to guarantee a bed for the night—first come first serve. You then needed to leave the premises, by a certain time come morning with all of your belongings. I was thankful to have gone to this place, where I could sleep safely.

Finally, on August 23rd, 1973 Mom pronounced those words I've longed to hear; "get ready we're going to pick-up the baby at Children's Aid." I don't recall questioning her about anything. I was extremely excited and eager to finally hold her in my arms! I had honestly thought this day would never come.

Mom never did inform me about what had happened, or where Christine went; the following three weeks after I left the hospital? She was very cold and barely spoke a word; something I was used to.

My sisters and I were ecstatic and jumping with joy. We finally got to take Christine home. She was our princess, who had returned to her mother! I took pictures with my sisters holding her. It was definitely love at first sight; snuggling and kissing her endlessly.

Now, off to meet Dave and his family! I was a proud mother! They too were in love with her! Gram gave a baby blanket as a gift. Again, I took pictures and had a short visit. It seemed like Mom was always in a hurry; cutting our visits short everywhere we went.

Everything was happening too fast; I didn't have much time to appreciate my baby. Go. Go. Go!

Mom had other places for us—to go to her friend Leona's house, which was about a forty-five-minute drive from Gram's. While living with Bernie and Mom on Santala, we played at Leona's place with her kids; they were friends of the family.

At least, I could admire my precious baby during the drive. I gently placed her tiny body between my legs, I softly spoke and caressed her little face and head. I uncovered her tiny feet and examined her long skinny toes; as she squeezed my baby finger. I was in admiration; she was perfect. I had something incredibly special!

I was under the impression, we were heading to Leona's to introduce my baby and have coffee. I soon realized this was to be a visit unlike another. I had a rude awakening; to why she was rushing everywhere we went!

Leona met us outside on arrival. I took a picture—I wanted lots of pictures with her on our first day. The one and most important person, who didn't have a picture taken with her, was me! This still bothers me to this day.

I remain grateful for the time I spent with her, showing her off like my little trophy. It would've been worse, if I had never seen her again; without any photos for souvenirs.

In the picture with Mom, she is smiling down at Christine. Today I can say, how dare her, knowing she'd never see her again! Or did she? I'll never know if she did, or if she had any updates from Leona over the years.

I was invited into the house. On the table as I entered, was an adoption paper. Mom insisted I sign it, along with everyone who was involved and was also pressuring me. What I didn't know; Christine was to be given up for adoption, to Leona's brother.

They were expressing how Leona's brother and wife could give the baby a wonderful life, a loving home and I mustn't forget, that she'd be spoiled rotten.

They emphasized how young I was— I was single, I wasn't completed my schooling and without an income. And everything my baby would need, ringing in my ears. What about my needs, why do I have to give up everything to please everyone? She was mine! She belonged to me! How I thought I could give her those things and spoil her rotten too; if I was given the chance to breathe, and think over this critical matter. I absolutely was capable of loving her more than anyone!

I was told before signing that Leona's brother was a pilot; had lots of money to spoil her, and had no other children.

The adoptive parents made me a few promises; they were to explain to Christine she was adopted, as soon as she could understand, they also made an agreement to give me news, and keep me updated through all of the important stages during her life. They reassured me, they'd send pictures.

I certainly didn't want to sign; Mom didn't leave me any other choice. She pointed out how I was underage, and how she was responsible for me. She'd threatened me with, "Don't make me have to call the police."

What are you responsible for? What a fucking joke! But, I allowed her threats to get into my head and I eventually signed that paper.

I knew I was fighting a losing battle. I had no chance in hell of gaining custody, everyone was against me. I don't remember the actual signing, but I do recognize my signature on the adoption paper.

Sad to say even to this day, I have no recollection of leaving my baby behind, leaving that house or even having to explain to my sisters, or anyone else for that matter. I've tried many times to remember, I have a complete loss of memory. I believe I have Dissociative amnesia, which is a disconnection and lack of continuity between thought, memories, surroundings and actions, which was caused by this traumatic event.

I had Christine wrapped in the blanket Gram had given. I figured it was meant for her from her great-grandmother, so I decided I'd leave it with her; with the thought it would pass on some warmth and love from someone special. I only remembered this, while having a flashback as I looked at the pictures.

Before, everyone involved decided to pull off the worst day of my life. Laura and I had everything figured out. I was to be a stay home mom; raise her until she attended prekindergarten. Only after I would've continued my schooling, or found a job.

Laura was going to continue school and work evenings. She was at least more emotionally stable than I was at that period of time. Of course, this was a vision, while we prayed for Christine to return to home to us. Laura repeating; we could raise Christine together, and I wouldn't be alone!

We excluded Mom from our plans, since she was cold, distant and never had a relationship with us. I had no positive support from any adult in my life, after leaving Santala Road. Mom had her own plans!

We certainly would've given Christine the most precious and essential things that life has to offer; love and protection. We knew exactly what a child needed. It was everything we were seeking, hoping and praying for, from our mother. We could've done a hell of a better job than she did with us!

Gram once suggested, I marry Jack to keep the baby, without having to sleep with him. I wasn't too keen on the idea; it did frighten me somewhat, if only she could've guaranteed I would marry Dave. Gram why didn't you insist? Why! You know I've always listened to you?

These are the ways from the *"baby scoop era."* Gram was trying her best, to keep the baby and the family together. Don't forget for the "baby *era*," you needed to marry to have a child. Maybe things would've turned out better, and more positively for everyone involved.

I'm sure Gram would've signed to be responsible for me. Gram knew how much we loved each other. She explained to me, when Dave would finish his education and obtain a suitable steady job, only then we'd eventually marry.

Mom made an appointment for her and me to consult a psychiatrist, at the Sanitarium of Laurentian University in Sudbury. I went a few times totally against my will. It's not surprising I didn't talk about my sexual abuse. I went in hope to make peace between us. Why now? No one has ever helped me!

> Many will come now to pry you open.
> I wonder what they will see.
> They will all come asking for the key.
> They will all come offering promises that the doubts will lessen
> flaunting their oaths as currency!
> Don't let them in. Anne-Marie Don't let them in!

I went along with the doctor's questions; answering to what I thought he wanted to hear. Mom told me she'd have me committed, because I was keeping too much to myself; she was now aware of my relationship with Richard and naturally I denied everything!

She took me for lunch at A&W; questioning me to see if it was true? I refused to admit what was happening. It was never mentioned ever again. I honestly didn't feel she cared, she simply said, if it was true to just put an end to it. She wasn't even upset or angry!

How could she even think I'd open up to a complete stranger; especially at the sanitarium? Oh no! I wasn't going to let her win over me!

It was so damn hard for me to continue with my life without Gram, Dave and their family after so many years.

> Many had assured me that they are not like the hurters
> they promised that their words were forged in steel
> they wanted nothing no rewards or fine gold

and they offered their ears and support just to seal the deal.
I cautioned myself. Anne-Marie
Don't let them in!

I angrily indicated to the doctor how absent my mother was throughout my entire life. And now she's hoping to have me locked up? She was the psycho one! I terminated my sessions!

I knew there were ears out there
Hard to find, but they are there!
They'll be ready to catch my tears
More than willing to show concern and care.
I am not about to hand over those duplicate keys
and again, I found myself at the very same spot!

Mom was asked to continue consulting, which she did for a short while. Unfortunately, it didn't change anything in our relationship, not surprising!

I can't say for sure, if she didn't bribe Leona and her husband Ron, to make an adoption deal somehow? This is one thing that will haunt me till the day I die! I've always said, and believed; she sold my baby for a house, or at least was offered a good price on it! I felt it was too darn coincidental, that she would want this one specific house, with all of the houses around. I was stunned to hear she bought that specific house!

I was also surprised to hear Dave and Paul had become friends. I wasn't aware they were buddies when we lived in Santala. My instinct tells me Dave was trying to get information on me, in a roundabout way. Nobody ever mentioned their friendship to me.

Dave filled me in on this many years ago. Asking if I knew he worked for INCO at the same place and period of time as mom. Nope! It was hard to comprehend why everyone kept all the information about him from me.

I thought it was kind of special, knowing Dave sat in the same kitchen where I was forced to sign the adoption paper. Also, the very last time I'd ever see our daughter. I've always said, "There's something fishy about this whole house story."

Mom stole my human and parental rights, while Bernie stole my innocence. Which parent was worse?

Who am I?
Where was that marvelous thing that so many children spoke about?
Who am I really?
Am I even the same?
I would love to enjoy my true self.
Be sure of who I am.

With Bernie we were forever walking on eggshells out of fear. With Mom we needed to be constantly on the ball due to all her secrets and keeping everything from us all.

There were no dialogs, or bonding whatsoever. She wasn't even our friend, which was just pathetic!

Mother, grandmother—please someone; explain to me how my mother could rip away the most precious thing I'd ever had? My baby! We spent many hours with her; I carried her full term for crying out loud, while being away alone in a strange city. Where was God when I needed him? Who was God anyways? Bernie said he was God, but in my eyes the priest was. But, how come God was not helping me? This was not my concept of God at all.

Why? Who gave her that right? Who? Why? Why would she hurt me like that? After all of those years of witnessing our abuses and she never had anything to say, nor did she have any authority over me. Who gave her the permission to do these terrible and awful acts of cruelty to me; I will never comprehend.

Even though she treated me like shit, I'd still buy her gifts in the hope of eventually gaining her love, or possibly just a friend. When we'd go out to bars, or to restaurants I paid for her, but never did I feel any gratitude.

I did go back to visit Bernie, John and David after giving birth. Paul had moved out west, to Nanaimo, British Columbia. Please, don't even ask me why I went back to visit, I was probably in search of a parent—how lost and confused was I? Maybe I wanted to see if he would own up that Christine was his child. Who knows? Maybe, I was expecting an apology too, I don't know. That obviously wasn't on his mind.

Probably hoping for something positive to happen, but nothing ever positive happens when it concerns Bernie. I gave him a hospital picture of the baby; telling him Dave was the father. For me it was essential, I make it clear he was not the father; I didn't need him harassing me. He was speechless!

He asked, if I'd like to go somewhere calm to discuss different matters with him? I hesitated for a moment, convincing myself I was older and it's been a long time since he hasn't bothered me. Praying he had changed his ways and I would be strong enough to stop him, if necessary. I agreed!

We went somewhere to sit on the grass near the water. I was incredibly stressed, alert and my guards were up. Things went smoothly for a while, until he told me, if I would go back he would buy me a car and a trailer to put my snow jet on.

My anxiety level instantly increased, almost to the point of paralyzing me. Once again, I felt fear running through my veins. He tried to kiss me. *Shit!!* He never learned from his mistakes. I finally got my nerve up and said, "No! That's enough! Take me back to your place." He did just that, and I left from there! I never went back.

Chapter eleven

In September 1973, my biological father and his mother had received news from my Uncle Edgar in Kitchener; saying I gave birth.

My dad spoke with Mom, stating they were on the way to bring me and Christine back to Quebec. They weren't aware my baby was gone!

They were extremely disappointed and saddened to learn, they were a couple of weeks too late. They still wanted to bring me, but mom insisted they take Laura and Jackie.

They returned a couple days later, giving them a chance to gather up their personal belongings. Now, another heartbreak—my sisters decided to leave me. I was left on my own, to deal with the enormous amount of hurt I felt from being abandoned; as my life came crumbling down again.

I didn't know if I was coming or going, but I sure as hell wasn't leaving with a stranger. I might've known he was my biological father, but I still called him by his first name!

I did keep contact with Christine's adopted parents, wishing them Happy Mother's Day, Father's Day, Merry Christmas and Happy Birthday to Christine. I called on a few occasions, but then their services were cut off. And, my letters were marked return to sender. Subsequently they moved; I grieved her loss one more time; they were nowhere to be found.

Afterwards I never did receive any news, or even one measly picture!

I tried gaining custody through a Law Firm in Sudbury; eventually he came to a dead end road as well. The internet was nonexistent in the seventies. It felt like they vanished off the face of the earth without a trace! Now, I had no chance in hell of finding my daughter.

After signing that one measly illegal adoption paper; I was forced to leave my baby in the hands of complete strangers. Mom, Gram, Helen, siblings and I never mentioned Christine for decades to come; making the event feel as if it was just a dream! Mom might have had updates through Leona; if she did I definitely wasn't aware of it. I was always in the dark with my emotions.

This specific event in my life was mostly a nightmare. I thought about the special place, for the evil people whom people call the non-believers. I don't want to say the word Hell, because I have already been there. But, if I didn't pull myself together, the world was only going to keep pushing me down. It was not going to get easier, if I kept playing the wrong beat.

Life was extremely difficult to carry on through, despite hardships and suffering; I was left with no choice, except to advance the best I could.

I found employment, as a waitress at a Chinese restaurant, on Notre Dame Avenue. I worked evenings and weekends while continuing school at Marymount College. Bernie came for lunch with John and David on a few occasions. I was always pleased to see the boys. I have absolutely no recollection of a conversation of any sort.

The owner would bring me back and forth to work; teasing and insinuating how he'd love to go skinny dipping with me. I'd tell him he was crazy and it definitely wasn't happening. One evening he said, "I'll bring you to my place." I assumed his wife would be there, since I knew her from the restaurant. He opened the door; cold chills spiked through my body, when I realized there was no one else present.

The place was bare, not one piece of furniture sat on the floor, with the exception of a bare mattress! We did not enter the apartment. I had this fear come over me, and I insisted he take me home, *now*! At that very instant I began cursing at him saying, if he didn't take me home I was going to reveal to his wife his secret apartment, and about his harassment towards me. That's exactly what he did. I quit the very next day!

Now, working at S. S. Kresge dining room and continuing my schooling I started to consume alcohol—going to bars to numb the pain. Finally, I found an apartment a few streets from Mom.

I'd go out with friends from work. Many times, I'd call Mom to get a ride to the Kingsway Hotel. She didn't mind, since she was a close acquaintance with the owner. She was pleased to do what she did best, entertaining the place, playing guitar and singing to make a couple of dollars. I repeatedly paid for her Tia-Maria's.

I drank rum and Coke; then two rums and Coke; straight rum, no Coke; then just a couple of straight rums. That night apparently the owner notified Mom to take her alcoholic daughter home. She did just that! She put me into bed fully clothed, in my one-bedroom apartment. I woke up with my face in puke and unsurprisingly my bed was full of the same. I was in a pitiful state of mind; only two months following my sixteenth birthday. As I look back on that period of time, it was clear to see I wasn't heading in the right direction. Where was my mother's support!

It's about time I started to be accountable for my actions. Due to my excessive drinking and passing out, I skipped a day of work and returned two days later. The manager, Christine and I had a discussion, "It's a few times now, you come in smelling like booze, if you don't do something about it, I will have no choice, but to fire you."

I was humiliated, but more cautious after that.

Another night
I smiled as I adjusted my make-believe crown.
It was time for me to go and see the crowd.
Let them know that I am around, if you know what I mean.
Head up. Head up, it's time to press play, girl.
Dressed in high-heeled shoes and the latest jeans!
I laughed as I thought bet, they didn't know that the villain is the star of
her own fucking play.
Did they even realize that I fought their battles for them?
But, they got the glory. Not even a fucking sorry.
It's funny how my story could easily spin out of control.
How quickly a queen can lose her throne.
Fuck! I thought I had everything.
A pocket full of money and the man of my dreams!
I have a blanket for the cold and the stars for the hard nights.

Out on the town with my friends, at the Nickel Range Hotel drinking, dancing, having fun and minding my own business, the owner came up to me, "Show your ID," My response, I didn't have it on me. He pointed out to my neighbour, who implied I was underage. I was asked to leave the premises. I'm sure this guy David had squealed on me, as a result of me not being interested in dating him.

I thought I was a smarty pants, I left through the front exit, and went back in through the back door. The owner spotted me, but didn't say a word. Next thing I knew, there were two police officers asking for my ID. I freaked out, and bee-lined it up towards the hotel rooms. On my way I turned around, believe it or not I was my own worst enemy—I started kicking them in the shins. Not surprising, they caught me and put me into the cruiser.

I didn't want anyone to recognize me in the police car; I slid down in the seat. Next I was brought down to the station. How embarrassing, I had to empty everything from my pockets. I was placed in a cell with a toilet without a seat, my comfort included a metal spring bed to sleep on; the worst was the door made of bars, and the guys across from me could see everything. I yelled like a hooligan, "Get me out of here! I don't want to be here! I want to go home! Get me out of here! I don't belong here!"

The other prisoners were screaming back, "Shut up! We want to sleep."

How could they sleep in anything, but their own beds? I continued freaking out until they let me out and told me to call my mother. She asked, "Where are you?" I answered, "At the cop shop."

She entered the station, and whispered, make it fast, as she had just made an illegal parking! I was appreciative of her for bringing me to my apartment. Was I ever pleased to be back in my bed? Most importantly, to walk free!

How lucky I felt to survey familiar ground again.
Be by myself once more.
Not locked up like a caged bird singing for freedom.
Freedom is a beautiful thing.

I didn't have to sit in a cell, thinking of the many things
I would do it if I had my wings again.
My chained restraints had been broken, and
I could now use my wings to fly,
Proving that freedom isn't a lie.

I could now ignite my loosened soul as
I flew past infinity and into eternity.

After putting off going out on the town for a couple of weeks, I returned to the Nickel Range Hotel, with my friend Carmen. We'd quietly be dancing together, and when the band would stop for their break, they'd usually sat at our table. We let ourselves get acquainted with them to some extent. The drummer was flirting with me. I began to feel important again! I was never bothered to show my ID.

On one of his breaks, he asked me to kindly meet him in the lobby. How dumb was I? He held my hand, leading me to the men's bathroom stall. I sincerely thought he was leading me there to talk. He started kissing me; I was filled with fear to see what was to follow, though it would be nothing I hadn't seen before. I wondered, *is this how relationships really start?*

He closed the door, dropped his briefs and placed his hands on my shoulders, forcing me down on him. I hadn't been expecting him to do this. I felt like running and screaming at the top of my lungs. But, at this point, I wasn't too sure, if that's how relationships are supposed to be, since all guys seem interested in sex alone. All but of course, with the exception of Dave who I could never forget!

I had no self-esteem whatsoever, keep in mind; I was a bastard good-for-nothing without even enough knowledge to tell him this was wrong. It seemed like I didn't know how to get out of these disgusting predicaments; living in fear and trying to satisfy everyone. I suppose that, subconsciously, I was reacting against my unhappy childhood. I was afraid to say no. In fact I had been taught that I could never say no. It was rude and it was considered answering back.

I just wanted someone to love; thinking this was my only hope. The drummer was having a house party. He asked me to join him at his place after work. I went, hoping to have some enjoyment other than fulfilling men's sexual fantasies. At the party, the women were after him like bees in a honeycomb. I felt like a kid! I didn't belong there. I was only a baby compared to the women, who were seeking his attention.

I didn't stay long. I escaped and never looked back. I never had any other interaction with him.

Carmen and I bar-hopped for a while; when we'd return to the Nickel Range, we never did sit near the stage, nor did the drummer bother me again.

Looking back on these incidents, I realize I was leading a vagabond existence; I completely gave up on family, home and possessions! I was a lost soul who simply was surviving; without a purpose in life.

I now started to slow down on going out drinking. It wasn't exciting anymore. I was still getting myself into trouble. I finally had enough; I realized I was hurting no one else but myself. I managed to save up for Christmas gifts to send to Laura and Jackie. I bought the biggest box of chocolate I could find on the market for the siblings.

Laura and I were both mourning the loss of our friendship.

Back left Mom's Dad John Matthews, Mom's mom Vicky (Pitre) Matthews
Edward Courtemanche Dad's father
Hector Courtemanche
Sally Matthews. Sarnia Ontario April 7, 1956.

Sally Matthews (17) Anne–Marie Espanola, Ontario.

Left Uncle Edgar Courtemanche Grandfather Edward Courtemanche Sally pregnant with Laura (18) Hector (21) 1958.

Me (1) Paul Mac Donald (2) in Sarnia Ontario in August 1958.

The One Room Schoolhouse,
#1 D Water's School June 1961.
Taken from, Women Institute of Lively Ontario.

Left Laura Anne–Marie
Mary Mac Donald with a family friend 1963.

Sheila Husson, our babysitter. This is to show you how poor we were. This is the only seating we had in the basement beneath the blanket were holes and the springs would scratch or pop up and pinch your skin. The kids would sit on the cold cement floor covered with ripped up linoleum Santala Road.

A view in the basement Sally (26) Bernie John (5) Mom Laura (8) the chairs would get destroyed due to Bernie's outrageous character. Santala Road 1966.

Florence (Grandpa's girlfriend of over 20 years) left Laura Mary Mac Donald Anne-Marie David Mac Donald
John Courtemanche 1966.

Florence and John Matthews left John Courtemanche (5) Margaret Mac Donald David Mac Donald (3) left front Laura (8) Mary Mac Donald (4) Santala Road Lively 1966.

Me when Bernie started to abuse me (7), Santala Rd. Lively.
1964 1965.

Arvo Basto (Dave's great uncle), our neighbour, kept us busy in the small gardens, plus huge gardens in the fields. We'd seed, weed and pick the crop when ready. His wife Aili would help us clean and cut the vegetables. We'd always had tea parties after our day's work was done. We played board games, Crokinole and Jumping Jacks; you name it we played it.
Mary Mac Donald front Paul Mac Donald John Courtemanche Anne-Marie
Santala Road Lively.

Lila Koski Anne-Marie
Santala Road 1964.

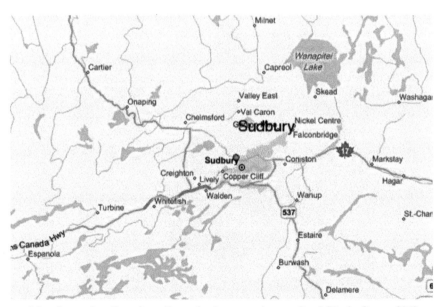

Map shows where I was born, Espanola, then some places we lived, Lively, Copper Cliff,
Walden, then Val Caron where the Adoption took place this is the proximity of Sudbury.

This is a picture of the Basto family farm, Eino Basto lived here on Niemi Road. We'd visit and have a hay daytime in that big hay barn on the right. There were many buildings on this huge property, example on the left to the house is a steam bath, where Finnish ladies would give birth from the Finnish community, due to the easy access to hot water, far left blacksmith shop, right a chicken coop, hay loft, then in front of us is the Pump house, with a huge open field between here and where we lived. This was the perfect place for ski-doing.

This is the exact Finnish costume Gram sewed for me for a grade 4 school project, with the little bonnet third down on the left.

At Grams, I could be myself and always felt safe.
My second home, being silly bugging Paappa ha-ha!!

Margaret Mac Donald (2)
Anne-Marie (10) Santala
Lively. Never without a smile!

Thanksgiving at Moms Anne-Marie right back towards the camera Mary Mac Donald
left John Courtemanche Margaret Mac Donald Andy Sue Powell Mom's best friend family
friend 1973.

We're on our way to celebrate our birthdays. Jack Basto
Sylvia Basto me
Santala Road Lively 1970.

Thanksgiving; Sally Matthews When she took the turkey out to put on the platter, the meat fell
off the bones, leaving her with just the skeleton 1973.

About 30 minutes after my friend Sarah brought her children inside, this bear along with her three cubs started roaming around their yard. This is to prove that the bears are still roaming free even after these many years in Lively 2019.

Sally Matthews (27) Bernie Mac Donald (40)
Red Rock Ontario 1967.

Grandpa John David sitting Sally
John and Bernie holidays with the three boys Red Rock Ontario 1967.

Sally Syble Matthews (27)
Red Rock Ontario 1967.

Anne-Marie Mac Donald Courtemanche & Sharon Dorival

Gram Sylvia Basto Jack Basto husband Paappa Aaro Basto August 23, 1970.

One of Sally's many parties after she separated from Bernie. At Annie Desjardins Camp where she spent a lot of time entertaining Mom 31–32 left with her guitar and wearing sunglasses.

This is the exact motorcycle I had at 14 years old.
1972-350cc Honda Gold wing

The Big Nickel is a 30 ft replica of a 1951 Canadian nickel. It's possibly the world's largest coin.
Sudbury is also the Nickel City of the world, the Dynamic Earth Museum in Sudbury 1976.

As of September 26, 2013 Frances Barrick Waterloo Region Record
WATERLOO — after 45 years as St. Monica House, a Waterloo maternity home for pregnant
teens is changing its name and making public its location.
The 20-bed residential home is now called Monica Place and on Wednesday, a sign was erected
advertising its existence at 231 Herbert St.
"We used to be a hidden secret," said Tonya Verburg, executive director of Monica Place.
"We are going to put a sign out front saying here we are for those who need us and we are not
ashamed to be here," Verburg said.

Christine Lynn Courtemanche Kitchener Waterloo July 29, 1973.

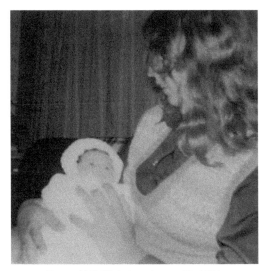

Laura (15) Christine, August 23, 1973.

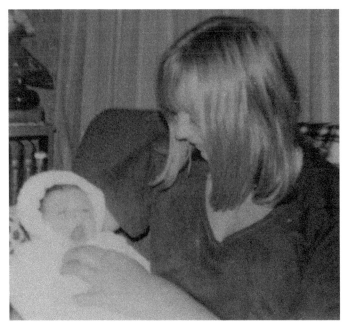

*Jackie Courtemanche (14) Christine Lynn
August 23, 1973.*

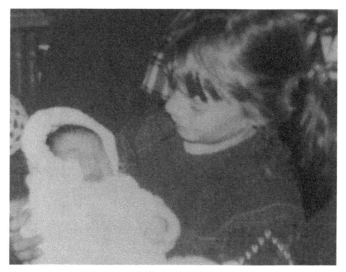

Margaret (8) Christine August 23, 1973.

Mary Mac Donald (10) Christine August 23, 1973.

Sylvia Basto Helen Koski Anne-Marie Christine. Santala Road. Lively August 23, 1973.

Helen Koski Christine
Santala Road Lively August 23, 1973.

Dave Koski (18) Anne-Marie (16) Christine Santala Road Lively August 23rd, 1973.

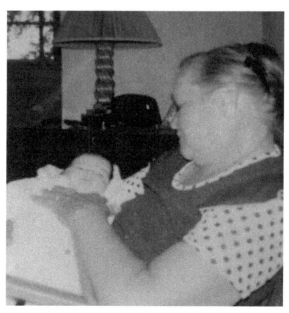

Gram Santala Road Lively August 23, 1973.

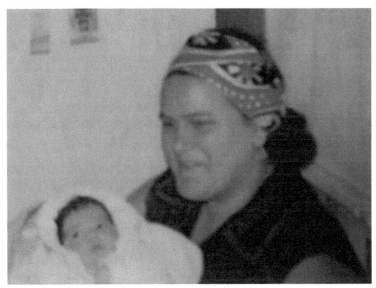

Sue Powell
August 23, 1973.

Sally Matthews Anne–Marie Leona Moreau
adopted aunt Val Caron District of Sudbury. August 23, 1973.

Chapter twelve

Laura has been hard at work, trying to convince me to move to Quebec. She emphasized on how enjoyable it was there. She was terribly concerned for me, and mentioned how useless she'd be if ever I needed her. Jackie now has moved back to Mom's. In May 1975, I decided it was time for a change, time for a fresh start with my little sis. I was excited to reunite with her and naturally to meet the other seven siblings, who couldn't speak a word of English. Thank goodness my father, grandmother and my step-mother Huguette did.

I was confused, underneath the mess of my thoughts; having mixed emotions, while leaving everyone I've ever loved behind. Having many fears and doubts about what lies ahead; it was time to take a chance on life. I was drowning and had nowhere to go! Things definitely couldn't get any worse. I suffered from severe separation anxiety. My heart was bleeding, and I eventually found a bit of comfort with my best friend Laura. We were finally finding some balance in our lives.

I must point out, for the first few days I was drinking heavily. Dad would wake up to a bottle of beer, so would I. We drank from sunrise to sunset. We kept this up for about a week. On one occasion I was proud of myself; I drank one beer more than him. One morning I woke up and kicked myself in the ass, *where are you going like this? There's absolutely nothing to be proud of!*

My anxiety suddenly hit me head-on—I was ridiculously reminding myself of Bernie. I was becoming way too much like the monsters, I really didn't want to become. So much booze!

I stopped drinking every day, and drank only on special occasions. I was really fighting to stay dry; the rain was pouring down inside. I was drowning in my silent tears, and dancing with my demons on my own.

I was coming to the end of my rope, and having a nervous breakdown. I was feeling extremely tired; it was getting harder to fight. My roaming thoughts kept me up at night. I thought about my failures, it was just the same familiar song playing over and over in my mind. Running away hadn't solved anything.

Unsurprisingly, I was in bad condition mentally. I was suffering from depression. I was a nervous wreck! Huguette brought me to consult with the doctor; he prescribed Valium. As I fell asleep that night, I heard all the words I longed to hear like love, need, forever and till death do us part. We are different, but the same.

My father unexpectedly grabbed and kissed me on the mouth, and took it upon himself to put his hand on one of my breasts. Finally at seventeen, I'd had enough of this bullshit. I found the strength from within and courage to push him away. I told him he had no right to do that! Dad, "I can do what I want, I made you!"

I thought this fucking world had gone to the dogs, and everybody was after one bitch. Fuck!! So much for my family! This was the first and last time he made any sexual advances towards me. I must say from that day forward I remained on my guard.

Huguette, had a few drinks at the neighbours, she wasn't feeling particularly good. She didn't handle alcohol well—after two drinks she'd be literally sick. This one time Dad followed her home, he slammed her head onto the ceramic countertop.

Every so often, he was just so hateful. This other time he broke her finger; he grabbed it and then *cracked!* This was simply because she spoke to a salesman who came to the door. He was possessive and dangerously jealous of her.

I'd like to share a few fun times. Laura and I were literally hanging out the dining room picture window. Huguette was sitting in the shade about eight feet below. Laura, "Go get me an egg. I'll give Huguette an egg shampoo." I dropped the egg! It cracked on her head; running down the sides of her head into her hair, Laura and I laughed hysterically. Huguette wasn't too impressed! She was insulted and implied how much it hurt. She eventually got over it and we laughed together.

Another fond memory was when Huguette needed my assistance with some footwear. It was springtime; she didn't have proper shoes to wear, so I lent her a pair. While walking downtown, she had slipped on a sheet of ice. It was hilarious, to see how her two feet flew out from beneath her. I started laughing uncontrollably bent over in two, I was sore from laughing. I asked if she was hurt, no! She insisted I help her to get up. I couldn't, I was too busy laughing.

The best part of this story was, a car stopped directly on the road, the driver got out, looked at Huguette on the ground and started to laugh, he then drove off. She tried getting up on her own, but eventually I needed to assist her. We laughed together, as time passed—what awesome memories we made.

Many times after supper I'd bring the seven siblings out for a healthy walk. My watch was broken; I needed to know the time, to have the kids back for their bedtime. We were joking around and having fun. I grabbed Huguette's Big Ben alarm clock, and dropped it into my ski pants. We all laughed—it was a hilarious moment. We'd walk about a mile down Lac Lapierre Boulevard; we turned around and continue our way home. The kids slept like babies after their walks. I appreciated the exercise, the company and the feeling of being free. These are the few awesome memories I have.

Another time Dad, Huguette and I were at the neighbour's and having a grand old time, just when Huguette said something that made Dad angry. His character changed instantly, like a switch had been thrown. This happened often for no reason.

He threw her out on the deck. I shouted at him, "She wasn't a dog to get thrown out like that." Oh boy! I didn't know my father; let me tell you I certainly got to know him pretty fast that evening. He tried to grab me, I went running down the hallway; I had nowhere else to run. He caught me and slammed me face-up against the wall; I was barely touching the floor. I screamed at him to let me go, he was squeezing the back of my neck. It was Fernand, the man of the house, who came to my rescue. He ordered him to leave me alone, boy I was relieved!

It was said my father didn't fight with men. He was known for being a coward; had the pleasure of beating women.

It was at Fernand's, I met my future husband, Daniel Richard. He was his nephew who came from Laval practically every weekend. There'd always be drinking and people coming and going. On quiet evenings Fernand, Daniel and I would play card games.

Daniel and I started going for car rides, and appreciated some quiet time. He was my only friend outside of my family members.

By the fall, my father was becoming explosive; he started to beat on Laura. He made a point of how much she reminded him of our mom. He'd punch her and slap her in the face; boasting how he learned certain ways to hit without leaving any bruising or marks, while training in the army. He'd pull her up off of the floor by her hair, as he continued hitting her, saying, "I'll make you cry." She shouted out at him, "I'll never cry for you." He kept punching her, until Huguette finally got the courage to tell him to leave her alone, or he'd kill her. Laura never did cry for him!

On a return from another night out drinking, Laura and I ran and jumped down the two stairs to our bedroom. We had been spending time with Huguette, trying to convince her to leave him. She deserves someone who respected and loved her. That's something we've definitely figured out on our own, from our experiences from Santala Road.

He claimed to have seen, and heard us jump down the stairs. He was furious. Before he stormed into our bedroom, I recall clearly advising Laura to squint and not to open her eyes. Otherwise he'd see the reflection of the light in them. He placed his two hands around Laura's neck, about an inch away. In a low voice, "You're lucky I can't see if it's you." He then turned around and walked out.

Once he left we cried, Laura's whole body started trembling. We realized how darn close he had been to strangling her. This just confirmed, we had a life and death situation in our hands. We had no choice, but to find a way to get Laura out of this horror house.

She finally arranged to get a ride to the underground subway train station in Montreal. A classmate's mother, who lived a few streets away, dropped her off at the north end of Montreal. Which is the second biggest city in Canada?

Later in life, Laura expressed how she was totally lost, heartbroken, crying, she was an emotional wreck; having no idea where she was going. She was left completely on her own to figure out which direction to go to purchase a one-way ticket back home to Sudbury. This lady literally saved my precious sister's life!

It was difficult to find someone to drive her; it was over an hour and a half drive. To make things more difficult, there weren't many people who were willing to get involved in other family's affairs, especially strangers. This earth angel offered her precious time during the weekday, while Dad would be gone to work.

When Laura had everything lined up to finally leave, she came to see me. She was exhausted, and shaking like a leaf! Urgently, "Anne-Marie I need your help, you need to give me money to take the train back to Sudbury?" I told her it was unfair to leave me, especially after we have finally reunited again." Another excuse I gave was, 'Dad calculated every penny I made from babysitting." Selfishly thinking, if I didn't give her the money she'd stay longer by my side.

She begged, stating she had no choice—that the next time he'd kill her. I knew damn well how things would've finished. We planned with Huguette's help, to cover-up the lies about the money. We were worried and nervous he would figure out our plan.

Together Huguette and we did our best to protect one other in every way possible. Everything panned out well. Laura and I cried endlessly—this was something we had dreaded—the ending for "us."

Prior to her leaving, she had major nervous breakdown. It was bad; she tried to commit suicide by taking a full bottle of aspirin. The ambulance rushed her to the hospital. The doctor explained, what had saved her life was the milk she took with her pills. Thank God!

We were again separated! We couldn't comprehend why we weren't able to be together. In all seriousness I realized now, I'd lost everyone I'd ever loved! I couldn't help but wonder, *Why me?* We were so close, but so far apart.

Life went on, as I continued to exist. I approached Daniel, and I asked him if he loved me enough to get married, otherwise I was following my sister's footsteps.

It became impossible to remain in the house any longer. I was drained; had no energy to run mentally, or physically, I needed a plan. I surely didn't want to move back to Moms. I had come to a dead-end road. I was surprised and thrilled Daniel said, "Yes."

The summer of 1976 Ron, dad's neighbour, came to offer me a replacement job for the summer holidays, at a sewing factory where he worked in Montreal. Saying, I didn't need experience, they had on the job training. I was thrilled to get out of the house! After work on Fridays, I would take the city bus to go meet Daniel at the office in Montreal. I had to walk a short way from the factory to the bus stop. Along the way, I noticed a non functional historical train station, and a man who was walking behind the building. As I turned the corner, he had his trousers down; he was swinging his penis in his hand and shouting, "Do you want this?" In a panic, I ran for dear life! I never looked back to see if he was following me.

Upon my arrival at the office, I was shaking and bawling. I couldn't believe what my eyes had seen. I had a difficult time explaining; I was so emotional—almost in shock. I was so thankful the man didn't follow me onto the bus. I've always been ultra-conservative with my clothing, but it apparently didn't make me less of a target. Many times I've asked my friends and family if they saw a black halo over my head, or something written on my forehead saying, "Abuse her."

Dad was just an overall miserable human being with the mentality of having control over everyone's life. Now, I realized, I'd left one crazy house to enter one very similar. What a world! When the hell and where was I to find happiness?

I had applied for unemployment. I filled out my cards every two weeks for a year. Back in those good old days, everything was done through snail mail—no internet. I found it strange, but Dad assured me I'd eventually receive a check. I never received one penny!

Dad would drive me around, so I could apply for employment. We stopped numerous times at different hotels for him to have a beer with the buddy's, and hopefully find contacts for his work also.

A few times I saw him kissing other women, while I exited the lady's room. I couldn't hurt Huguette, by letting her in on the terrible situation I had witnessed. Again, I was curious to know what a normal healthy relationship was.

They finally separated, she now informed me, and Dad was opening my letters and deposited my checks into their bank account. I did call EI, but it was too late to do anything—a few years had already passed.

Leading up to my wedding I continued taking the bus on Fridays; I'd return home the same evening when Daniel was finished work.

My plan to get married didn't stop Dad from flipping out with his jealous fits, and calling me a bitch, slut, no good for nothing. I honestly don't know what he was thinking in his sick twisted head.

There was another unpleasant time; he, Laura and I were visiting Grandma, who lived next door. Dad was loaded as usual; he was talking badly about Mom in a degrading and demeaning way.

Like always, his mother agreed with everything he said. She was frightened of him, with his hot temper. Laura and I defended Mom, although she had never defended us. We said, it wasn't fair of them to be constantly putting her down, since she wasn't present to defend her-self. Never did Mom say anything negative about him; she always told us, once we'd get to know him and only then we could judge for ourselves, what kind of person he was.

I was getting so fed up with talking in circles. I wanted to leave the conversation; I got up to go to the washroom. He grabbed my arm, twisting it, and angrily shouted at me, that I couldn't go anywhere. He pushed me back down into my chair. His fingernails dug into my skin, I was bleeding! I was pissed off and insulted; I didn't want to make a scene.

He was angry after all of this time, I called him by his first name the first time we met! "Well yeah, it's kind of normal—you were a stranger to me." Now, in my heart and soul, I felt he didn't even deserve that honour—to have the title Dad.

Like a little child, I asked for permission to go to the washroom and he said, "Yes." Afterwards, I snuck out to go home. The next morning, while we were sitting at the breakfast table, he noticed the lesion on my arm. He was curious and asked what happened, I snapped at him, "You did it." He had no apology for me. He just replied, "I don't remember." Yeah right! In so many ways, he was just like Bernie!

I am not sure if a good alcoholic exists, but he was definitely a bad one. I just put up with it, as I was soon to be married!

Daniel and I appreciated our moments together, for one and a half years. Which panned out to be around four and a half months we've dated?

Chapter thirteen

I literally can say, Daniel saved me from this place of torment. I was tired of running away from my problems and from all of the toxic people. Our wedding was held on March 12, 1977 at the Church in St. Lin. It was the first bilingual ceremony performed. Our three children were later baptized in this gorgeous church.

Present were Daniel's parents, his three siblings, Huguette, Dad, my seven siblings and a few aunts and uncles, along with a couple of cousins. We had an extremely small reception. At the house were alcoholic beverages, lunch was followed with a cake Mme Leblanc Mme Chausse gave as a wedding gift.

For my entire life, I had envisioned Laura being my maid of honour. It was now hopeless due to Dad's abuses to her. I would rather have had a loving compassionate mother, who would have been honoured to be by my side, as I would've of her. She never asked me one single question about my wedding; I didn't bother to invite her. It was a bittersweet day for me.

I never had the honour of being spoiled with a wedding shower, or any baby showers. My entire life was built on dark dreams, with the worst nightmares. Happiness wasn't meant for me!

Together Daniel and I had three beautiful healthy children, who were born in St. Jerome. Our first Annie! I spent a month in the hospital during my first trimester due to vaginal bleeding, which was the outcome of a rough vaginal exam, performed by a general practitioner. Subsequently, I was dilated to three centimeters. Next, around eight months pregnant, it was essential I stay off my feet. I was fragile and experienced blood loss. But, I obeyed the doctor's orders not to trigger a premature delivery, or any complications.

I was experiencing contractions every two minutes for sixteen hours, and the doctor decided to induce me. Dr. Tanguay cut, cut and cut; Annie entered this world on May 23rd, 1979. When I delivered, I was dilated to only seven centimeters; weighing 6-lb-12oz.

Junior was born on April 18th, 1982. I was having painless contractions. I decided for reassurance I'd go for an exam at the hospital. I was thankful we went; I gave birth, fifty minutes on my arrival. I was short of having a home birth, or a car birth. On my arrival I was already dilated to seven centimeters.

He was six weeks premature. His birth weight was 5-lb-10oz. It was required to place him in an incubator; he was blue. When he was discharged his weighted went down to 5-lb-2oz. The pediatrician emphasized on how critical it was to feed him every hour. He was drinking, one-quarter of an ounce hourly. It was clear, if he would skip one feeding; it would be vital to admit him to the hospital.

We made an agreement with the pediatrician to follow his orders. We did well, but were exhausted. Doctor McLellan expressed, he would've been an eight-pound baby, if I would've carried him to full term. He was a fighter!

While in the hospital I took advantage of the situation, to have a painful cyst surgically removed from my wrist, which was growing by the minute.

Now, for Joey! Again, I was dilated at three centimeters at around seven months. Except this time, it was necessary I be hospitalized. His weight caused tremendous pain, and problems with my veins; which also caused false labour. The doctor prescribed elastic pantyhose for pregnant ladies to wear until the end of my pregnancy. After being hospitalized for three weeks, I was sent home with bed rest ordered. The two children were great helpers around the house…

At 3 a.m. I went into pre-labour and my membranes ruptured in my sleep. We finally made it to the hospital! In the labour room I revealed to the nurse my baby was ready to get out. Her response was, "I just examined you, you're not ready quite yet." I then let out a shout, and made it clear the baby was crowning. She obviously didn't believe me, as she was bringing in the wheelchair, to have me taken to the delivery room; she saw the baby's head. Funny, how fast she advanced; pushing the chair! She ran to open the doors; calling out for Doctor Champagne!

There wasn't time to make it to the delivery room, or even transform the bed into a delivery bed. Joey had decided *ready or not, here I come!* I gave birth at 9:24 a.m. in the labour room. With Doctor Champagne literally, lying across the foot of my bed stitching me up!

Joey was my heaviest, weighing 7-lb-13-oz. Surprisingly, he was put in the incubator— his sugar level was too low.

I had three miscarriages between my pregnancies. I've always had difficulty carrying my babies during pregnancy—I carry extremely low. They would be positioned directly on my pelvic bone, causing lower back ache.

Again, I took advantage of being at the hospital. I needed an operation on my foot. I had a plantar wart that was stubborn and didn't want to part. I'd had it burned with liquid nitrogen, cut out a couple of times, but it always came back. This time, they cut deep, and then stitched me up. At the same time I had my Fallopian tubes cut and burned, through my belly button. I was in pain everywhere; being sewed up in three different places, ouch!

In January 1980 when Annie was eight months, I had a cholecystectomy, along with an appendectomy. I was recovering in my room, when suddenly nurse Vezina, happened to peep in. Apparently, I was as white as a sheet. This angel of a lady later faithfully expressed how she felt blessed to have been at the right place at the right time! She hurried to take my blood pressure, all I can remember hearing, was a voice pronouncing, "Twenty," I lost consciousness. My next recollection was waking up on the operating table. The doctor was taking out my stitches. I spoke out, "Hey! I'm awake. Do something!" I then saw the mask come over my face.

I was transferred to the ICU and hooked up to every possible machine. I finally regained consciousness; I was lost and confused to where I was. There was a lot of noise, coming from the numerous machines, and lots of motion happening. The nurse explained I was in the Intensive Care Unit; I was doing better, telling me to stay strong. She also mentioned there was an ailing man who just passed away. I don't remember anything else after that. I lost consciousness for the next three days.

I was hemorrhaging internally! Nothing was flowing through the drainage tube. I received three units of blood; I remained, ten more days. The doctor who operated, Dr. Joseph Lemire happily indicated, this sort of incident was exceedingly rare. He truly thought he was going to lose me.

He did express how I gave him a scare! I joked and said, "You probably forgot the scissors or something in me." He laughed! I was losing weight by the minute, he ordered the nurse to give brandy before each meal for a week; once again, to open my appetite. I had lost thirty pounds in one month. My appetite had completely vanished.

I was excited, but exhausted to finally be home with Annie, Daniel and my sister Mary who had come down from Sudbury, was absent from school; Mom sent her down on the train. Naturally, we paid for her round-trip fare and for her helping hand. She returned home, a few days following my hospital discharge.

The next devastating event in my life was, on Saint-John the Baptist Day, June 24, 1980. Which is Quebec's national holiday? We'd spent the gorgeous day at Daniel's aunt and uncles. It was a scorching hot day! We spent most of our time relaxing in the swimming pool, had supper, and got home around 10 p.m.

Huguette called, implying her and Dad wanted to come for a coffee. I found it odd, this was the first time they'd ever come at that time. I made it clear, Daniel was heading to bed shortly; he worked in the morning. She assured me they wouldn't stay long.

When they showed up, their faces were white as could be! The serious-ness of the matter showed on their faces. My instant reaction was, "Oh my God! Did someone die or something?" There was absolutely no reaction to be found! Once, in the kitchen after a few minutes, Dad wasted no time; recommending he speaks with me, alone?

He placed his hands on my shoulders, while trying to explain; my mother was involved in a terrible tragedy and succumbed to her injuries. With a force I didn't know I possessed, I pushed him away from me. My two hands on his chest; lashing out at him, "It is not a joke to play on me." He broke down, and cried loudly.

Huguette joined the choir, which confirmed his story. A few minutes later the phone rang. Paul was calling to announce the catastrophe. Explaining, they had been trying to reach me all evening. With no cell phone, or caller ID we had no idea people would be trying to contact us.

Mom died shortly after 4 p.m. at the beginning of her evening shift. She worked for INCO International Nickel Company. This was a mining disaster. She was the first woman to be deceased in a mining accident for INCO.

Mom was only thirty-nine years old, and a single mother of eight. We were devastated! Huguette and dad watched Annie for a week. I advised Huguette to never leave Dad alone with her. I didn't trust him, but neither did she.

She loved Annie so much; we had confidence in leaving Annie in her care. I also knew with the seven siblings Annie would have plenty of attention and love. She was their live doll!

We packed our luggage, along with Annie's; we went our separate ways. I bawled from St. Lin to Sudbury, which was an eight to nine hour drive. By the time we arrived, I couldn't shed another tear. It was the longest trip to Sudbury we'd ever done!

I had jotted down a list of questions for my mother. I had been hoping she'd be honest enough to answer them in July, when we were to go up on our summer holidays. Unfortunately they were never answered. Let me start question; #1) What time was I born? #2) Was I an accidental pregnancy? #3) Did you ever love me? # 4) Why did you let Bernie constantly abuses the five older kids, sexually, physically, or emotionally? #5) Why did you always push me towards Bernie and Richard? #6) What's your excuse for leaving me behind with Bernie? #7) Why did you ignore Laura when she asked you to bring me with you and the girls? #8) Are you proud of each decisions you made? #9) Why couldn't you accept and help raise Christine? #10) Can you tell me the truth? Once in your lifetime, did you sell or get a deal on getting the house in exchange for my baby? #11) Did you ever visit Leona when Christine went to visit them? #12) Did you ever receive in any way whatsoever any news on Christine over the years? #13) Why did you send me away to Kitchener, when you should've helped me like any other normal mother would have done? #14) Do you even have a reason for hating me so much? #15) Why couldn't you discuss my pregnancy with me instead of going behind my back and making all decisions without my consent?

Dear Mom,

There were so many questions that were spinning through my head. So many questions you have left unanswered. Like, why did you treat me in such an awful way, but never had the guts to say. Why'd you leave me and run away? You left me alone in my puddles of tears with my heartaches, cares and fears. Did you really have no idea how damaged I was? Yet, you left me standing there to pull myself together? How come you never asked me how I was coping? How come? My life was in shreds, but you left me, alone-with him-with them to pick up the pieces. My heart was broken when I realized you'd played me like a clown, leaving me to put on a show. A play where no one was smiling, if they were laughing they were laughing at me. I hated myself and inside I just wanted to die. Did you know that many times I stayed up late just crying? Other times I wondered, if you'd miss me if I was gone?

Eric Clapton-Tears in Heaven https://youtu.be/JxPj3GAYYZ0 made me cry time after time, as I would think of Mom. I'd wonder if my mother would recognize me, or pretend she didn't know me, if I saw her in heaven, or would she even talk to me, or would she be that same mean person she was on earth. Would she hold my hand, if I saw her in heaven, or would I say till we meet again; wondering could she really be in heaven?

About one year following my cholecystectomy, and blood transfusions, I was contacted and needed blood work done. Apparently, there had been some contaminated blood used. Now, something else to worry about! The doctor's office contacted me, requesting I go in for the results. I demanded she tell me on the phone. She replied it was against medical policy. Now, my imagination was working overtime thinking of the worst-case scenario. Why wouldn't she just say over the phone, if it was negative?

The doctor confirmed negative, everything was good. So, why couldn't the secretary just tell me instead of getting me all worked up? I didn't have HIV! What a relief! It would've been just my luck!

Another shocking news concerning some health problems; I've been dealing with for close to a year. After doing many blood tests, and having another anesthesia for another thorough biopsy; as they needed a bigger piece of tissue.

Now, came the moment of truth. In May 1988, I was diagnosed with cervical cancer. I had received a couple of Laser treatments, but the cancer was still growing. I wasn't given any other option, but to have surgery. I was operated on at Montreal's Sacré Coeur Hospital and discharged after seven days.

Laura came to give me her tender loving care, and help us with the kids. Naturally, she brought along her three children. The two youngest, Kristen and Joey were toilet training. That meant when one went, the other one surely had to go. With only one potty Laura said, they'd have to learn to wait each their turn. This became incredibly challenging. Laura was very patient, and the four other cousins played amazingly well together.

I had a hysterectomy. I was having the urge to urinate often. Laura kept insisting I stay off my feet—to lie down on the couch, she presumed I was getting up too often. She was right! I started to have blood spots; bigger spots and it seemed like every half hour, I felt that urge to go to urinate.

I began passing blood clots. In only about thirty minutes, the clots would start getting bigger and thicker. Laura called the neighbour's daughter to babysit the kids. Meanwhile, her mother placed a blanket on the back seat of her car. I was hemorrhaging!

We arrived at the hospital in St. Jerome, in about thirty-five minutes. The nurse approached Laura, asking her if she was comfortable washing me? Laura glanced at me, I uttered if she was comfortable with it, so was I. It was an awkward moment. I was in agonizing pain and getting weaker by the minute.

I was at the point where anyone could have washed me. The emergency doctor contacted my gynecologist Dr. Desaulniers, in Montreal. He insisted I'd be transferred; ASAP.

I travelled in the ambulance with a registered nurse; she'd shake my shoulder every time I'd close my eyes and repeat, "Don't close your eyes stay with me!"

Laura managed to get Daniel to meet her in St. Jerome. They both drove behind the ambulance. She later explained how she thought they'd kill themselves; Daniel wanted to arrive at the same time as the ambulance. She remembers the visions; following us with the sirens, flashing lights, while passing traffic.

As for myself, I remember the loud rattling sounds coming from all directions inside the ambulance. The nurse was shouting to the driver; "hurry up I think we're losing her." I felt secure in her presence! My concern was having a blowout and losing control, or someone cutting us off; we'd definitely kill ourselves!

I was losing even bigger clots now, about four to six inches round and about three-quarters of an inch thick; at times a little bigger. I'd have one about every fifteen to twenty minutes. By now the clots were huge. I'd now warn the nurse when one was coming. It was similar to contractions followed by a mini baby. The hospital in St. Jerome installed an intravenous, but they didn't put in a PICC line for a blood transfusion.

Once we arrived at Sacré Cœur Hospital, I had the doctor on one arm and the nurse on the other. It took many attempts each, before the doctor finally found a vein. He explained how it was difficult to find a vein, when a person loses a lot of blood! They kept apologizing, for pricking me so many times. I was full of bruises. I received five units of blood within twenty-four hours.

While I was in the ER, a priest went to another patient to give the last rites. Laura and I were in shock. I can still picture Laura's face! She kept an eye on him, telling me he'd better not come to my bedside, or she'd freak out. I vaguely remember someone asking if I was a Catholic and inquiring if I wanted my last rites. Except, due to the amount of blood I lost, I remember just bits and pieces. So exactly, what I answered, or whether I received my last rites, God only knows!

I was then packed with gauze, which is called a vaginal packing for hemorrhaging. The bleeding finally stopped! Two days later they removed the packing and an ultrasound was performed to see where I was hemorrhaging from; no trace of blood!

I spent another nine days in the hospital. When I finally was discharged, it was essential for Laura to return home, to get her children back into school.

I want to personally thank the doctors, nurses, the ambulance technicians, nurse's aides and everyone else I may have forgotten, who were involved in saving my life. I am blessed and will forever be grateful to Laura for her kindness of compassionate care; she easily gave to me, and my family.

I separated from Daniel in February 1989. Unfortunately, things didn't work out between us; I did my best with the knowledge I had. I believe we did an amazing job in raising our three children. I will always be thankful, for giving me my three awesome children.

He was a great father, always present in their lives. His personality was mainly on the reserved side. I'm assuming, it was in my best interest at the beginning of our relationship. But, as time went on; I was in need of more love and affection. I am definitely not pointing fingers. This absolutely doesn't make him a bad person. I needed validation!

I can say, in twelve years of marriage, I don't recall him ever saying he loved me of his own accord. I'd pronounce those three words everyone wants to hear, I love you, and he'd respond, me too. After a while I stopped telling him.

After our breakup, we stayed on the friendliest terms for the kid's sake. I found an apartment next to their school. It was perfect; they kept their friends and school.

Due to the mental trauma, sexual and physical assaults I had injured, I was granted an annulment of marriage. The procedure was I go to the cathedral in St. Jerome, to disclose the names of a couple of witnesses to our marriage. I furnished them with all contact information necessary.

A Catholic marriage can be annulled; if a tribunal's investigation determines the union was lacking certain essential elements, before vows were exchanged. It was necessary I make an appointment at The Ecclesiastical Tribunal of Montreal.

I wasn't capable of loving a man at this time in my life; I was still running from myself. I had respect for Daniel. I just wasn't in love with him. I was miserable; I wanted to break free somehow. I needed to gain control of my life, and restart over again.

I have no doubt he loved me in his own way; though I can't speak for him. I don't wish him any harm. On the contrary, I wish him only happiness.

My life was catching up to me now at full speed! I needed to think more of myself, to try to heal from damage to everything, and everyone did to me. I was lost and in survival mode for my entire life; feeling trapped in my own body.

For me, the most important thing in my life were my children, they always came before me. I did my absolute best to give them the most important essentials of life; love and compassion. I made sure they were spoiled in every way possible. I took motherhood very seriously!

Laura and I reunited in July 2010, when I moved in with her. As usual we'd discuss our childhood and express how damaged we were.

Once we reconnected to our feelings, our emotions we'd grieve, cry our hearts out; we'd embrace then appreciate each other's presence. We would rarely talk about the abuses, until our next visit. This mainly occurred on the first days of our visit.

We never went into detail; it was way too painful to awaken those emotions. We've tried many times to comprehend how or why Mom was so cruel and heartless. We felt we were the only ones around who could understand one another's pain and suffering. We were each other's emotional strength!

On a few occasions, Laura wanted to tell Daniel about the abuses. I'd get upset, and warn her, she'd better not. Saying I'd be so resentful and angry if she did. I wasn't ready to tell him, or anyone else for that matter. It was my life and I'll tell whomever I chose; whenever I feel the time is right!

Sad to say, but in twelve years of marriage, I never found it in my heart to let him in on my enormous secrets of the abuses, nor about the baby. I confessed to him years later, once I laid charges against Bernie.

It was ironic, I could keep the secrets and pain from him for so long. I carried this massive weight around that's been holding me down my entire life! I had a hard enough time personally dealing with it; let alone tell the whole world, at that point in time. Actually, I never dealt with any of it; I buried them with my thoughts.

After about three years of being a single mother, I met Horace Leblanc. We lived common-law for seven years. I admired him for not drinking!

Eventually, his mother fell ill; we brought her into our care for a year. I was working full time, and when I'd get home; she'd be excited to see me after spending her long day alone.

I'd prepare her meals, so she didn't need to use the stove; a zap in the microwave is all that was needed. Better to be safe than sorry. She was a companion.

Her son was jealous of our relationship. He has issues with her; he treated her harshly. They argued a lot, I always took her side; as I have always defended the weak. I enjoyed our time together; shopping and eating at the restaurants, etc.

He started to display aggression towards her. Things started to escalate fast; I asked one of his brothers to find her another place to live. I explained to him what Horace was doing; I wasn't comfortable being around him anymore.

He didn't have time to find her a place. She fell ill; it was necessary for her to be hospitalized. I went to the hospital to bathe her, as she didn't allow anyone to wash her, but me.

By the time she was discharged the brother managed to get her a low rental apartment, for the elderly. We explained to her, she had a new place; I wasn't going to be with her son for much longer. She understood, but was very saddened. I did visit her a few times, for reassurance. Her happiness was one of my responsibilities. She never held back, telling me in front of her son; I was too good for him. How rare is that for a mother to say?

She had been operated on for the pancreas; was on medication. When she'd eat it went straight out into the toilet—pretty much instantly. One school morning, Joey walked out of his room; straight into a pile of poop, which was sitting on the kitchen floor. He was furious, but kept his cool, as he had great respect for the elderly. He told her nicely to please be more careful, because it wasn't pleasant to wake up and step into poop! He handled that situation like a true gentleman, at nearly twelve years old!

Please don't get me wrong. Horace and I did have some good times. We had many weekends camping with Junior, Joey and his kids at Mont Tremblant. We'd swim, fish, climb trees and slide down from mountains on a rope, which was tied to a tree at the top and the bottom.

On this particular day Horace and Joey were at the top getting the rope ready. It was essential he made the proper knot. Looking around, enjoying the view, waiting for Joey to pass the gloves; suddenly he saw something pass from the corner of his eye. His natural reflection was to swing out to grab it, thank God he did; it was my Joey! He'd slid on some green moss and just couldn't stop!

I was with my video camera; I let it fall and started to yell from the top of my lungs "NOOOO!!!!" Let me tell you, words can't express how grateful I was when he caught him in mid-air! My baby was safe!

They finally made it down safely. I can assure you, I was done with these slides; never again! It was the scare of our lives, something we'll never forget; I can guarantee, never will he!

It was now time for bunion surgery on my left foot. Some said it wasn't too painful. Yeah, right! That was the worst pain ever! I couldn't descend my foot to the floor, the pressure was ridiculously too much to bear; the intense pain lasted over a month.

Around two months following my surgery, it was time to freeze my big toe to remove the stitches along with the two removable surgical pins. They were needed to stabilize the bones in the correct position, which was followed with the removal of a lump of the bone. This did help take some pain and pressure away.

I came to realize, if ever my other foot needed the same operation; it would be a cold day in hell before I have the procedure done again!

Laura finally made me promise to seek professional help. To deal with my childhood abuses for once and for all. I had always expressed to her I was fine and I didn't need help. The truth of the matter is, it does eventually catch up to you, sooner or later. I just wished it would've been sooner!

I consulted with a social worker about ten times. After my first session, I felt the sudden urge to go to Sudbury, to press charges against Bernie. At every session, I'd become more and more emotionally depleted.

As expected, they stirred up many undesirable memories. I started getting flashbacks; when these memories would resurface, it would hit me like a brick wall. I would get extremely overwhelmed with anger and guilt; then cry like a baby.

I had finally reconnected with my inner child! It wasn't easy! I can't even get close to describing the immense amount of pain, and panic I felt from deep within. This anger suddenly gave me more strength and courage to get revenge. It was high time; I saved that little girl that's been buried within for so long!

When I finally felt confident, and gained enough self-control, I literally asked her, if she was ever abused? "No! She answered." I immediately told her, I didn't need her services anymore. I stopped my session's right there and then. My perspective of her was very cold, emotionless and had no compassion. She'd ask questions then jot down everything; asking me to hold my thoughts, in order for her to keep up with her writing.

Chapter fourteen

April of 1991 I made arrangements, just-so my children were safe and well taken care of. I then asked Laura if was ready mentally and physically to team up with me. I had a boost of energy, and was in full gear to press charges against Bernie; the sooner the better. Her immediate response was, "most definitely in a heartbeat." She expressed that finally he'll pay for his actions. She wasn't sure she'd be able to make every court hearing, as it might be difficult for her to part from her eldest son's bedside; he was battling non-Hodgkin's Lymphoma cancer at thirteen years old.

He pulled through an exceptionally long hard chemotherapy regime, with lots of prayers; support from family, friends and the people in their small community of Gold River, on Vancouver Island. She always arranged to be present in court.

We knew how important this was for one another. I certainly couldn't have done it without her! We were in this together, I absolutely needed her by my side, we were one—we were a team!

Amazing news! On June 30, 1992 officer Larry Dénommé, placed Bernard Mac Donald under arrest. When he read the charges, his response was, "Not again they accused me many years ago and it didn't get them very far, just like now."

On July 15, 1992 there was a bail hearing, along with conditions and promises to the court. As a surety to attend court he provided collateral worth $20,000.00.

This still wasn't time for my separation; I was still relying on Horace. This was extremely important! It was necessary, I preserve my energy to concentrate on what had been eating me alive my entire life. I had always wanted to face Bernie, and to bring him to justice; expose him for the monster he is; proving to the world this did happen. It seemed as if nobody believed our story. My worst fear was he would die before paying the consequences of his actions.

Laura, Jackie and I became private detectives; we had a one-week delay. Bernie was going to disprove he had one testicle. This was something I remembered so well. While filing a police statement, the constable asks victims to describe a mark, a tattoo, or maybe a scar on the abuser that very few people would know about. You'll be shocked over how this particular bit of evidence ended up.

When the last three weeks of our trial were approaching, two of our sisters stepped forward. Although they were not interested in laying their own charges, they testified to what they remembered.

One of the girls was Bernie's youngest daughter, Margaret. We were immensely proud of her, for finding the strength and the courage to testify against her own father? She announced she hadn't received even a spanking growing up. She also testified to what she had seen happening to us, along with the atmosphere of fear, even she was exposed to.

Jackie also was an amazing witness; she testified, she saw Bernie abuse me through a hole in the wall panel; between the two bedrooms. I also remember peeking through it. At times we couldn't see. On the parent's side, the view always depended on how the clothes were hanging. These two witnesses, without a doubt strengthened our case.

Laura was my strongest and main witness. She was amazing. I can't emphasize enough, on how proud and blessed I was to have her total support. Susan told Laura she was tremendously proud of her, pointing out on how solid she remained throughout her crucial testimony, which was used as evidence towards Bernie's crimes.

We were all grateful to our sisters for speaking up. Supporting our efforts, for once and for all to get justice for the damage he has caused to our family.

I never held it against any of my siblings, who couldn't find it within themselves to come forward. We all have our own healing process, and we were defending our entire dysfunctional family. We knew it was high time Bernie paid. Together we stand as one!

We also had been supported, by a group of women in the courthouse, who truly believed in us. They gave us the courage and strength to carry on, without ever giving up. These amazing women were by our sides from day one up to the very last day of our process, and the judge's sentencing.

When I first saw our crown attorney, Susan Stothart, I have to admit I asked for her age—she looked like a teenager. She had just graduated from law school. She had no experience in sexual abuse cases—we were her first clients. I must be honest here I was scared and had my doubts. I was in this to win!

By the time we finally made it to trial, she had a couple of sexual cases under her belt. This young lady expressed how this case was so important to her. She was immensely confident; I must mention also how determined she was to win this case. Our young lawyer was incredibly pleased, with us witnesses also hopeful, but most importantly, she honestly believed in us; it was plain to see.

She stated how challenging it would be to convince the judge of Bernie's crimes, since he came from a good loving family. We heard through the grapevine, due to his upbringing, he didn't believe sexual abuse existed in the world.

All through my pregnancy with Christine, I did my best to remain positive. I adored this tiny human being growing inside me. I always said it was Dave's. I can't deny there was still that wee possibility; it could still be Bernie's. If she would be his, my motherly heart could never change.

I surely tried my best to get on with life. I was surviving doing the right things; barely making it through life, pleasing everyone to make myself look good, as though I had everything together. I was covering up my shame, hurt and guilt. It never occurred to me how I was forgetting myself.

We had a long dragged-out preliminary hearing and trial process. Surprisingly, I started speaking to my deceased mother. I was still pissed off and furious with her, but I begged for her support for once. I'd sadly expressed how she hadn't been any help to me in her living life. Now, she was gone; I prayed, if it was possible to find it within her heart, to make justice for us here on earth!

Bernie wasn't admitting to anything. This judge had tried two sexual abuse cases before ours, and acquitted both defendants. One even had a witness the accused had confessed to; he still got off!

Our crown attorney was preparing us for the worst-case scenario. The Victim's assistance group was saying, if this judge does not convict on ours, they'd never bring him any other sexual abuse cases.

You can imagine the sick scenario Bernie's lawyer was bringing up. The trial brought out even more shocking discoveries about Bernie that were hard to believe.

Throughout this long trial, we had our ups and downs. At one point we asked the Court martial, if we could take pictures. He replied, he didn't see a problem, if court wasn't in session.

We purchased a disposable camera; the next day at court we got a few pictures of the courtroom. All I wanted was a picture of Bernie. I convinced Laura to get one as he walked in. Done! I thought he looked like the devil! I wanted to show everyone; they'd see for themselves!

Now, we were in trouble! Once the judge entered, he addressed the court about our camera; if the offender was in the pictures, he'd call a mistrial. Someone had reported that we had taken pictures, and of course reported it to his lawyer, who naturally didn't waste a minute submitting it to the judge.

Well it was the moment of truth? When the judge called a recess, officer Larry was requested by the court to have the pictures developed. I can proudly announce, all of the pictures were black. To this day, I'm not a hundred percent sure whether that was true; or he was protecting our case. We were relieved. All we could say was, thank God!

Let's put that behind us, we had something serious going on. There was an argument about Bernie's testicles, I swore he had only one; I was sticking to my story! I knew this was crucial evidence to our case; to prove me wrong he swore he had two.

Susan called a recess. She and Laura were scared we'd get a mistrial; if ever the judge had even a slightest doubt. They were telling me, "Anne-Marie you were young! Maybe a bit confused! It was a long time ago!" I stomped my feet getting upset; crying out of frustration! I kept saying, "Why don't you guys believe me?" They were repeatedly reminding me of how young I was, when the abuse took place! Telling me it's okay, if I changed my mind. No way! I maintained my assertion! He had only one testicle!

I asked Susan, if it was possible, to make a request to the judge, to bring in a neutral doctor. I insisted it was absolutely essential to have him examined. This definitely was a substantial piece of evidence to our case. She said, "Wait one minute I'll be right back!" I had given her the best idea ever.

She came back, and claimed she had spoken to Bernie's doctor; there was an ultrasound performed on Bernie. She had good news and bad news; bad news for us, he had two testicles! Good news for us, one didn't descend into the scrotum! This was the most amazing news yet! I felt like we had already won our trial! This now gave us more fighting power; we were not giving up!

We hugged, cried and jumped for joy. What an amazing fast-thinking lawyer we had. Any doubts about her, have downright vanished! She has won my respect and confidence. The three of us were relieved one more time. We made it through another stressful close call for a mistrial. Our nerves were running scarce! I forgave them for lacking trust in me, or they thought it would be best to say, I was mistaken and too young; to save us from any possibility of a mistrial?

Obviously, they wanted to be safe, rather than sorry. But honestly, I could not do that. I understood their point of view not wanting a mistrial. But, of all Seriousness, do you think I did? We had come this far, we pulled ourselves together, we're not giving up. I have waited all my life to see this day!

Again, we almost had a third mistrial. The judge wanted to call a "Stay of Proceeding," meaning it had taken too long from the preliminary hearing, to the actual criminal trial. We were getting pretty worked up now, to the point of being pissed off. We were afraid to lose our case, due to some stupid technicality, or minor details.

Seriously, you can't imagine how terrifying this was! I certainly didn't want to give Bernie that satisfaction. We hadn't come this far, for the trial to end unfairly.

Again, we had our ups and oh boy did we have our downs! Laura and I remained strong, while doing our best to remain calm; we never gave up hope, nor on each other. It wasn't our fault at all—Bernie would change lawyers, another didn't have time to know the case before court date, or the other was a conflict of interest, as he had been Mom's lawyer a few years prior.

It seemed like they had every excuse in the book, to delay court appearances. I must now emphasize on how I thought we had the best lawyer ever. She proved to the judge, we were always ready, including the explanations about the costs I'd incurred in flying from Montreal and flying Laura in from Vancouver all expenses paid. The outcome, we resume the trial! We were saved once more.

All through the preliminary hearing, and the court trial, Bernie showed no remorse—he denied everything. While I was testifying, he tapped his pencil on the table. The judge demands he stop, he continues until the judge commands Susan to remove it from him. She managed to take it by pulling it, as far as possible from him. She played safe and smart!

She mentioned how she felt bad vibrations and insecurities around him, even with the judge and the courtroom filled with people.

Bernie was still trying to intimidate me. I tried to ignore him; lowering myself on my seat. I couldn't stand to see his devil face, while I was testifying. I didn't need him trying to influence my testimony in any way!

We three sisters had a week break to complete our private investigation, as the judge called a stay. We came up with my daughter's whereabouts. We gave all the information to Larry; he continued his private investigation.

He came back with some great news; she was married with three children, one boy and two girls. Christine and her husband were working in the Canadian Forces in Valcartier in Quebec. That's all the information Larry could come up with.

Larry did locate our housekeeper Miss Cooperman, who was living in a long-term care facility in Sudbury. He paid her a visit he sadly said, the only thing she had to say about working at the house was, "bad house, very bad house, bad situation, not good," as she had dementia, along with a very strong German accent. It's amazing even through her illness that she would remember that!

Unfortunately, Laura also brought Bernie to court for his crimes against her; the charges were acquitted. I can't even imagine how crushed she must have felt, along with feeling ridiculed. My heart bled for her. This was just so unfair. We all knew damn well he abused my little sister. After being a victim of him in childhood, she had been victimized over again.

Ironically, the truth is what acquitted Bernie of her charges—the truth, she couldn't see his face in the dark under her blanket, performing oral sex on her six-year-old body. This was absurd, we were outraged!

The defense lawyer stated Bernie now suffered from phlebitis in his right leg, high blood pressure, a deteriorated disc in his back, asthma, bronchitis and needed to take seventeen different pills daily. He added that there had been no further evidence of bad conduct since that time. He told the judge. "You ought not to punish conduct that occurred twenty-five years ago as if it occurred today."

Bernie admitted to the court, he might have had intercourse "just once, not more, if it even happened." We all know he said this only because we had found my daughter; he feared a paternity test might reveal he was perjuring himself.

His lawyer suggested Bernie be sentenced to less than two years, and ordered to perform community service. He also said Bernie had put in fifty years of productive work, and had raised several children.

Susan wasted no time, in reminding the judge that the court was dealing with a man, convicted of sexually abusing his stepdaughters for eight years, and constantly for six, at age seven, oral sex and digital penetration; at ten, performing sexual intercourse by placing the victim over a workbench and having sexual intercourse on a regular basis. She stated that these are "some of the most serious forms of sexual abuse that can be perpetrated on a child. Long-term, highly intrusive sexual abuse by stepfather, coupled with violence in the home, plus threats." Bernie had been arraigned on four counts.

Finally, on February 20, 1996 after five years of going back and forth to the preliminary, and then to the Supreme Court of Canada, the judge sentenced Bernie. I then started shifting the guilt from him to me. Our lawyer was asking for three to five years. She told us not to expect much.

The next day, the Honourable John Poupore needed only five minutes to deliberate on a sentence. As he announced it, I sobbed quietly, as I held John and Jackie's hands. I was petrified to hear Judge Poupore pronounce those two words, Not Guilty!

It was unfortunate, Laura wasn't able to attend the sentencing, which was one of the most important days of our process; she was waiting impatiently at home, to hear my voice pronounce, GUILTY!!

"Having regard to all the circumstances in this case," intoned Judge Poupore, "the nature of these offenses, the repeated acts, intimidation by the offender, the breach of trust by the offender, the lack of remorse and irresponsibility shown by the offender, lasting harm to the victim and society's need to deter such conduct, this court sentences Mr. Bernard Mac Donald to five years on count number one and three years on count number two. You, Mr. Mac Donald, remind us of Paul Bernardo and his horrific crimes, therefore, you are going to be sentenced to Maximum Security in the same prison, Kingston Penitentiary." The third count was merged into count number two. In all there were three of my charges, and the fourth was Laura's.

The sentences were to be served concurrently, and Mr. Bernard Mac Donald would be eligible for day parole after serving one-sixth of his sentence. The judge made sure he went to the maximum-security penitentiary, which is for sentences longer than two years and one day. Larry explained to us, when they bring an abuser to the prison, they open the doors; state their full name, announce their crimes and then close the doors.

Once the trial was over, journalist Terry Fender, Jackie, John and I went across the street from the courthouse for a good coffee! I was thankful it was over, yet I had some mixed feelings, happy and sad; tears of triumph and sadness, along with tremendous sense of guilt; I had put a man in prison?

I appreciated taking a few extra days to decompress. I met with a lawyer to apply for compensation on my behalf under the Compensation for Victims of Crime Act. I had learned about this from our support group. This was something new to me, but it was worth a try. My application resulted in a hearing before the board. If I wasn't in agreement with the proposed award, I would have to travel to Toronto to have an oral hearing before a two-member panel. This is what the Board wrote:

> *The Board recognizes that no amount of money adequately compensates victims of crimes for the injustices that they have suffered, but also finds the quantum of this award to be reasonable within the context of the compensation for Victims of Crime Act R.S.O. 1990 C. 24, as amended and generally in keeping with other Board decisions pertaining to injuries of comparable nature and severity.*

I was awarded $10,000.00 and after I paid my lawyer fees I received $8,000.00.

I seriously had no energy left in me to contest. We all thought, it was still an exceedingly small amount for everything I had been through. I wasn't doing this for money, but for my own healing and to encourage others. If I was eligible for compensation why not, maybe others would be too. It doesn't take the pain, and lifetime suffering away, but for me it was a sign of recognition and validation in the eyes of the law. I believe it should be the abuser who should be obliged to pay.

He served twenty-two months; then discharged a few months earlier due to good behaviour. What a small price to pay for robbing us of our lives. He did admit to some of the charges, while receiving counseling during his incarceration.

I came to realized, Bernie earned every minute of his imprisonment. I must say it again! He needed justice served to him before he passed away, and also for our healing. If I had known there was plenty of support I would have done it years sooner.

Throughout the trial, and once he was released, it took me many years to grasp the fact that he couldn't harm me anymore. That's how much mental control he had over me, even though he wasn't physically around; I've always felt the need to look over my shoulders. There were times; I swear I saw him in another car. We'd drive around just to lose him; we'd soon realize, it was my anxiety playing games on me out of fear. I thought I was going insane!

I finally got a grip on myself; I started to take charge of my life. The timing was perfect; I separated from Horace in July of 1998, which was long overdue.

For many years, Laura felt guilty about leaving me behind. We'll never know the reasons why Mom did that.

Some say you must remember, your mom was a victim and was beaten by him for years.

She was probably scared, he'd come after her; just maybe she left me behind to placate him.

I've always thought these were the most ridiculous excuses ever, as there are no acceptable excuses in the world, anyone could possibly ever give me that would satisfy my conscious. She wanted to be free of him and I was her ticket out!

I want people to know, I am no longer a victim. I am a survivor! The victim is no longer my name for I am no longer a slave to fear. This world is filled with hate, so many can relate to it. Life is unfair and victims are expected to deal with its realities, while living under the label. What can you do?

I encourage, anyone who's been through sexual, physical, or even emotional abuse, to seek justice for their own healing and growth. Change for the better my friends. Push on! Don't stay in a corner trying to remain invisible. Don't accept your fate as a blessing.

They won't like that you are fighting back. Let them know, you realize there is more to life than thinking about sex and pleasing men.

You no longer must put on an act. Your body is yours to do as you please. I know your mind still feels trapped. As for me I still wonder, why my mother never woke up to the pain that I went through right under her nose. All her lies were just to save her sorry ass. And look, who was left to pick up the pieces. Did she ever care for me? So many questions still needed answers.

Chapter fifteen

My next relationship began faster than expected. In August 1998 Horace was taking his sweet old time to move out! I gave him one more week. I needed him out, before starting on my next relationship with Stephane Brun. He expressed to me, he would wait as long as it took! He was an industrial machinery mechanic from the pickle factory, where I was working. He was aware of my personal situation, and had a discussion with Diane Desjardins, a co-worker; implying he'd never hurt me! We all made arrangements to meet for breakfast on Saturday.

Stephane and I made it, not Diane. We started a serious discussion, about what we were expecting in a relationship. I was kind of hesitant, considering he was eleven years younger, even though he didn't look or act it. He was extremely mature; asking if I would be interested in dating him. I say yes! The other employees encouraged us. He had a son who was three and a four-year-old daughter. He had brought them around to the factory many times—they were sweet kids. He was a great guy—we had worked together for eight years.

After dating for about six months, I had a working accident. I literally sliced my hand open, with a glass gallon jar. I tried to take the cap off, but the top of the jar broke with it. There were long and short zigzags of the glass jar that remained attached to the cap. Suddenly it slipped off, and I jammed it in-between my index finger and the thumb on my left hand, there was a pool of blood.

My friend Diane later told me, they needed to clean up my bloody mess! The foreman Jimmy rushed me to the hospital; he was driving on the shoulder of the road. He was also the only person in the company, who had a first aid certification. He taped two sanitary pads like a sand-wich over my cut, and then secured everything with tape to slow down the bleeding.

We made it to the hospital in about fifteen minutes; the blood-soaked up the pads. You could literally envision my pulse in the blood. The vein and muscle were cut!

Annie was called to join me; Jimmy needed to get back to production. I was relieved to see her! Nine days later I had surgery on my muscle. Stephane offered to take care of me, help around the house with boys, including the meals. He has now moved in for good!

After a few months I started my occupational therapy, which lasted a year and a half. I was unable to even budge my thumb.

Stephane was well-liked and accepted by everyone. He was a great help in time of need! His family also loved and accepted me into their family, with open arms.

We moved Annie to Sherbrook to attend school. She took nursing; she realized she wasn't made for nursing! She switched to hairdressing, which she enjoyed very much.

It was during this time, I took my nurse's aide course. I succeeded! But, it was necessary I returned back to the factory, until I could find a job in healthcare.

It took about one week, following my course to land myself a full-time job. I quit the full-time factory job, and I returned on my days off, if they needed extra help.

I had always dreamed of being a registered nurse. To take English nursing in my area, I would've had to move to Montreal. At this specific time, I wasn't motivated enough to follow my dream, I also didn't think it was the best choice to make with young children.

I must say, I adored my job as a nurse's aide, and furthermore I would have never given it up for anything. Jaclo Residence was a private long-term residence. It had thirty-nine beds and four rooms, St. Jerome Hospital rented for their patients; we were responsible for their care. It was perfect for me, full-time night shift. There was a huge difference in the pay, compared to the public long-term health care; it was perfectly satisfying for my needs. My family was more important than money; I felt the need to be present in their lives.

I worked there for a year. Unfortunately, it was necessary to relocate all thirty-nine patients. This was extremely hard on everyone. We had no idea this was going to occur. We had a staff meeting on a Saturday; we were informed they were closing the residence, as it had been sold! Everyone needed to find another place to live before Tuesday? Tears were spilled on each shift from families, employees, as well as the patients. No one had a clue where they were going!

This was an emotional and pitiless situation. They were my family away from home, which I absolutely loved. I did go visit a few of the patients, once they were settled in their new places. I wanted to be sure they were well and content in their new homes.

Living the life of a health care worker, we aren't supposed to personally attach ourselves to the patients. I don't know too many caretakers who can.

Junior attended Vanier College in Montreal, while renting an apartment within walking distance, with three brothers who also attended the college.

Stephane eventually bought another car, and gave his Ford Focus to Junior, so he could come home on weekends. That saved us trips to Montreal and back.

Stephane and I decided to purchase a house in Sainte-Sophie.

I started at a new place as a nurse's aide, again in a private long-term residence. Since it didn't consist of many hours, I found another job. Joey was in senior high, working weekends and evenings at La Belle Provence restaurant, he wasn't around very much.

Stephane and I started to argue and fight a lot over his children. They were getting older and being more demanding I questioned Stephane, "Why do you get your kids, if you're not present for them?" He worked seven days a week, he also had two jobs. His kids did pretty much what they wanted. They were forever testing their father, as most kids do.

There were things I disagreed with, I tried to explain how I felt; at five and six years old they should be asking to go into the fridge. At least express what they wanted before just helping themselves to anything they desired. There were things for everyone's lunches, including items Joey would buy for himself; plus taking forever to close the door.

I honestly didn't want to keep denying them everything. They'd be playing hide and seek, I'd explained to them; other bedrooms were personal, private and needed permission to enter. They would complain to their father saying they weren't allowed to do anything in the house, sad to say he would get upset and we'd argue.

Stephane always had the perception; I was attacking his kids, which was ridiculous. I've always said, I love all well-behaved children. Not little monsters! I was trying to educate and teach them. In life there'll be different rules to follow, it is important to have manners and respect the values for others—that there are limits and values to learn in life.

Unfortunately, Stephane let his kids get away with a lot. My perspective was, he felt guilty that he wasn't around enough! I'm sure most men do with their children—they don't want to pass for the mean parent.

In the fall of 2006 I had a biopsy done, on a huge nodule on my thyroid, the results came back negative! The nodule kept getting bigger by the minute. In October, the Otolaryngologist specialist decided to remove the right lobe. On the operating table he took a second biopsy—still negative.

I was now recovering at home; before I knew it, I received a phone call, stating the specialist absolutely needed to see me as soon as possible! I was in the office the following week.

The Otolaryngologist explained the biopsy performed on the table had gone to pathology; it had come back positive for Thyroid cancer. Now, I need to be reopened! I ended up with a total thyroidectomy.

My second surgery was performed one week before Christmas. The incision from the first operation was far from being healed. I was having ulcers, which were caused from an allergic reaction to the silk dissolvable sutures; used on the interior layers of skin. I joked with him saying he should open his fingers. He laughed explaining, he'd make an incision just below the present one.

Six weeks following my first surgery; I was sent to St. Luc Hospital in Montreal, to receive radioiodine 131 treatment. Everything was covered in plastic; the telephone, desk, table, pillows, mattress; the bathroom floor was covered and taped with soaker pads. This was a lead-lined room. It was fascinating to see. It was the last room down the hallway. There is only one room like this in this huge hospital. I kind of felt special being here.

My meals were placed on the half-door of my room, since no one was allowed to be near me. I was radio-active. The nurse had joked, saying I would almost glow in the dark. Radioiodine could be harmful to a healthy person. I was left totally on my own and no visitors from family, friends, doctors or nurses or nurses aids.

When I was discharged, I sat on the back seat; the most distant as possible, while I leaned against the door.

I remained in my bedroom. I wasn't permitted to touch, share any food, or drinks with anyone. It was essential I flush the toilet three times, due to the nuclear medicine that was released from my body, through biological elimination, and sweating. Stephane and I slept apart for a week.

By the end of January, I was placed on Synthroid for life, which is a thyroid hormone replacement medication. Without this pill I wouldn't exist. It controls my body heat, hunger and mood, also it regulates my heart, digestive system, muscle control, concentration, and it maintains the bones and my fatigue.

Before my diagnosis, I was voraciously hungry, it didn't make sense where I was putting everything I eat. As for my fatigue, it was extreme. I found it essential to stop everywhere for a snooze, on the side of the road, even when just a few minutes away from home. I'd fall asleep watching TV, which definitely wasn't in my habits. Whenever I had the chance, I'd sleep! My concentration was extremely poor. How many times did I pass my turn-off coming home, or going to work? At the catering, I would have to calculate. I couldn't even count to one hundred! When I stopped my count; I'd have thirty-odd items. I told Marie not to put me in any calculating position, until I get some blood work done. I'd be having a conversation with someone, and next thing you know they'd tell me, I was repeating everything I'd just said, two minutes prior. This was happening all of the time!

I'd break down crying and upset; I wasn't conscious of my repeating. Bawling in front of my poor kids, who felt hopeless? "Mom, you need to make an appointment ASAP!" I honestly thought I had Alzheimer's disease.

These are just a few little examples of what a sick thyroid can do. The doctor said, I was so infected and swollen he had a hard time seeing if he removed everything!

With my second operation, I lost my voice. When I spoke I'd have to yell, yet my voice would come out as a whisper. This gave me a terrible raw throat trying to speak. The specialist had notched my vocal cords; he couldn't guarantee I would get my voice back. Thankfully, it finally came back, about three months later. I couldn't imagine myself going through life like that.

I spent Christmas alone that year. My kids went to their father's to celebrate. I sent Stephane to his mother's family supper, which was literally five minutes away. I just wanted to sleep. I surely wasn't up for visiting. Stephane was kind enough to bring me a plate of supper, which I barely touched, as I was vomiting.

My second operation was very painful mentally, physically and hard to recover, due to the fact of having two operations one after another? I caught pneumonia and I was given antibiotics intravenously, which kept me in the hospital a few extra days. I was at my weakest. It was necessary to have blood tests every three months, to find the closest dosage of hormone replacement, so I could lead a normal healthy life.

It was necessary to have a whole-body scan, in nuclear medicine, which involves the injection of a radioactive tracer called technetium, which is a procedure that's done to check for metastases. I had this procedure done twice in the first year and then once a year for four years. The last one was in 2016 and it still showed a little piece of thyroid tissue that was left behind.

This procedure was also done to reassure, the small thyroid tissue stayed dormant. The internist insisted I stay in treatment for hypothyroidism, not to wake, or activate the cancer within the small tissue; it is dormant for now, Praise God!

I finally made it back to work. Sylvie, a co-worker and I continued to acknowledge the many abuses that were present in this private residence. There were a few patients in their fifties, who were unable to live on their own.

One patient told me, the male caretaker on the night shift was abusing her, and was buying her silence with a carton of cigarettes weekly. He also gave her extra meds, to make her drowsy during the day. The owner was aware of this abuse; she did absolutely nothing!

There were extra mattresses leaning up against the walls in the hallway. They were placed into the rooms to make extra money. As a result, the residence was overcrowded to a dangerous extent. My biggest fear was, if ever there'd be a fire; many innocent patients would be killed due to the owner's greed.

In these specific rooms, these innocent patients couldn't walk or talk. In certain rooms, there wasn't enough space to care for the patients; without a chance of injuring ourselves.

Some patients were tied to chairs and in their beds, while given other patient's pills that weren't their prescription. At times we were given orders, not to change the patient's dirty diaper; something I couldn't do. There were families, who couldn't afford to buy adult diapers. I think she just wanted to show she was the boss and was in charge; at the cost of the patient's well being.

We knew the families visiting habits; we'd be ordered once again by the owner, to untie them before the families arrived. There were patients with scabies, so I reported it to the owner. She didn't even bother looking at anybody. The residence was totally infested. I gave her names of certain patients that needed immediate medical assistance, due to bedsores deep enough you could see their bones. Others had scabies, different sores and infections. The doctor came once a month, or for emergency calls, which I've never seen. The owner made her own list, of the order of importance of treatment. She also made sure she was present when he saw each patient.

I went to my co-worker and told her I couldn't continue working and pretend nothing was wrong. I felt it was my civil duty to defend these poor helpless people. I felt obliged to report these abuses! She said; she'd stick by me all the way. I filed complaints to the Quebec government's office, I was sworn confidentiality.

The government sent nurses to verify the situation—it was bad. We reported everything, hoping they would write notes, report all of the negligence and abuses that were occurring in this home.

The nurses ordered a disinfectant crew, many nurse aids, a couple of social workers and extra nurses, to get this home back to a safe and healthy residence. All residents and employees needed to have double treatment for scabies.

A dump truck was sent to pick up all of the personal clothing and bedding. Everything was put into huge orange garbage bags and then taken to Joliette Hospital to be disinfected, which was an hour's drive away. This whole procedure took almost a month and a half.

The head nurse was still trying to gain control of the situation, she went to our boss and spilled her guts, repeating everything we had told her. So much for remaining anonymous—we were fired! Fired for defending and protecting the innocent! I had worked there for three years. My friend Sylvie was the owner's sister-in-law; worked there for eighteen years.

The boss took action against us; we received a subpoena to appear in court. It cost us four thousand dollars each in lawyer fees, for protecting our elderly. I was so grateful to have had two of the patients transferred before all hell broke loose, and I wasn't allowed to enter the residence.

I returned to the government's office about six months later to advise them; the same night worker was still drinking and the situation remained the same. This was confirmed by other workers I've kept in contact with. This incident was televised on the TVA news in French. The government said they couldn't do anything about the abuses, since it was privately owned, also the fact it has been operational for so long. How disgusting! We were so angry! We couldn't believe we had lost against this monster. It took me a very long time to get over this particular situation; knowing I couldn't save them.

The monster tried to convince the unemployment agent; I had sworn at the residents and didn't change them when necessary. I cried trying to clarify; the one swearing was that same evening-night worker.

I loved them, and wouldn't ever harm them in any way whatsoever. This was so heart-breaking I sobbed! I missed them dearly; prayed they'd all eventually find a much better caring home. I had no choice, I quit my second job.

The unemployment agent gave me the benefit of the doubt, after insisting this wasn't in my character. I advised them to send inspectors to verify what was happening in this residence.

Before I was fired, I did explain to the many family's how the owner was mistreating their loved ones. I expressed how vital it was to keep a close eye on their beloved. I strongly encouraged them to please find a new home for their loved ones!

Some family members were too frail themselves to take action. Others assured me they'd come around more to make sure their relatives weren't being mistreated; they no longer announced their visiting time. Some patients were afraid and refused to complain, because they believed they'd be out on the street with no other place to go. Almost everyone involved with these patients were naturally concerned and very comprehensive.

My friend Sylvie and I had done our job, as health care workers. We are to protect and defend the sick! If I had to do it over again I wouldn't change anything; except to report this situation earlier.

I took a well deserved holiday. I needed time to process, and try to put this horrible event behind me. It was essential I think of my well-being. I needed to pray for those vulnerable people, and also pray for those helpless patients that were left in that monster's care. This took a toll on me!

After about six months, I found another job in health care, not far from the last place. I was hired on the spot. The owners of this residence were aware of the mistreatment happening in the other home. They were awesome; they were compassionate and caring people.

This Residence George Franc was affiliated with the public long-term care facility. At the beginning I didn't have many hours, so I found a second job déjà vu! This time at a catering, Les Ailes Du Palais, I worked here, until I had a full time position at the residence; it took nearly three months.

We all know that's not very healthy for any relationship. Stephane and I continued to drift more and more apart. He decided it would be best to end our twelve-year relationship.

Chapter sixteen

We sold the house! I needed to get away from all of the chaos, the timing was perfect! Along with my three kids and Annie's spouse Martin, we planned our trip to Vernon B.C. for Laura's son Richard's wedding. We all pitched in to cover the total cost of everything. The ceremony took place on the famous date of 7-7-07 such a beautiful church ceremony and reception.

We flew out from Montreal to Edmonton; stayed at Laura's overnight, and then we drove through the gorgeous Rocky Mountains. In Vernon we spent a full week with Laura's three kids. We rented a huge home with a spa, trampoline, walking distance, so everyone could go to the beach, rent a sea-doo and go to restaurants and bars. We ate fresh cherries every day. Imagine everything was perfect. The temperature never went lower than forty degrees Celsius.

At the house we had ping-pong tournaments. Laura and I showed the kids a great time. This was life—an amazing family reunion. Very relaxing, and exactly what I needed! That week flew by very quickly; we headed back to Laura's in Camrose, Alberta, and made more awesome memories.

On my return, reality hit me; I desperately needed to find a new place to live. My appliances, furniture and personal belongings were put into a storage unit. I will now need to move two times!

I have the most wonderful support group ever, my kids, Martin and a few of their close friends. I'm so blessed to have such loving, caring and understanding children who never judged me. They encouraged me, during the most difficult times in my life.

I moved in with a co-worker, Denise Dagenais, I lived with her for a few months until my apartment was vacant.

In the spring of 2010, I was helping her move into a bachelor apartment at her daughter Karine Melancon's place. We were just about finished, when I thought I was on the last step and fell. I sprained my ankle pretty bad, but held onto that silly box for dear life! I was brought to the hospital; soon I had a cast up to my knee. I removed it myself after about three weeks, the worst decision ever. I suffered for about a year—even the weight of the sheets hurt.

Laura and I decided I could move in with her and her husband for a year or two. I didn't want a cast on when arriving in Alberta; I needed a job!

I told my kids my stay was temporary. Annie proudly announced she was pregnant. She was waiting until I arrived at Laura's; such an exciting secret to keep for so long. Once she'd announced this amazing news, I didn't feel like moving anymore.

The fact was, Laura and I had made numerous plans; we were looking forward to spending our precious time together; I couldn't turn back just yet. My vehicle was being transported on the train from Montreal to Edmonton; I received it two weeks later.

In Camrose, I obtained a job in long-term care at The Bethany Group, one month following my arrival. As usual I landed myself a second job. This one was at the Catholic Social Services; working with intellectually handicapped adults.

We were anxious to finally be together for more than two weeks. When our children were young we weren't able to see one another, for sometimes up to five years at times. The prices to travel were just outrageous. We each had single income households. Our jobs were the best, and most rewarding; stay home moms!

During our one year together, we celebrated our birthdays, Christmas, Easter and more. Our last celebrations of anything together were when we lived on Santala Road; Laura thirteen and me fourteen. This was an amazing magical year for us; a year that passed too fast. I'll forever cherish spending these precious moments together.

I moved back to Quebec in July 2011. I was unemployed for a year; recuperating from working the many doubles, along with mixed shifts of two jobs, I was exhausted!

There was no rush to find a job. I helped and bonded with Kelly-Ann, who was Annie and Martin's brand-new baby girl; my little princess!

They came up with a wonderful idea. Me owning and operating a home daycare! They explained to me, they'd purchase a house; I would pay rent. I must say, Annie was an amazing help; she did all the advertising and set up a Facebook page. We shopped for toys, playpens, a changing table and potties; Martin made sure there were security gates he also arranged to have the yard fenced in within a couple of weeks.

I went to obtain a city permit, and took some short courses on how to run a daycare. I thought this would reassure the parents of their children's safety and well-being; along with teaching requirements for each different age group.

We were ready for the grand opening. I moved in on a Sunday; opened on Monday. Kelly-Ann was thirteen months old. First to join us was a family's little boy Thomas. By the end of the week I had my six children's spots filled. This is the maximum number of children allowed in-home daycare in Quebec, with one adult.

I had five toddlers under fifteen months old, along with a three-year-old girl Emma. She loved to lend a helping hand with her brother Sam, who was my youngest. Elly, also was a great helper; I could use all of the help possible.

When it was lunchtime I'd give each a spoon full on their turn. I realized that by the time I returned to the first, Leakim would be sitting with her mouth wide open. They were incredibly patient, as they watched one another take their spoonful. They were truly adorable! I can't lie, it was challenging at times.

After a couple of weeks; I figured I'd let them eat alone. I'd just wash my floor after lunch instead of at the end of the day. We celebrated their second birthdays together, along with Emma, who had her fourth birthday with us. It was always pleasant to have Ari Kim, Junior's future wife, come to lend a helping hand, and to have an adult to converse with.

As much as I loved the children and having Kelly-Ann with me every day, I started missing my nursing job. I applied at the hospital in Lachute; I was thrilled when I received that one phone call from Stephanie Pomminville from Human Resource, announcing I was part of the team!

I needed to give the family's notice of the closing of the daycare. I was returning to a passion of mine; nurse's aide! Naturally, on each of their last days, we cried together including Annie—we all had an incredibly special bond; we were family! I'm blessed to have contributed to their growth and early development, in one of the most important years of their lives. I am also very appreciative of Annie and Martin for this awesome opportunity!

Following Dad's and Huguette's separation, she moved to Montreal with her children. Dad kept the house, and soon met Gisele. After living together for nearly two years; he decided to sell. They moved to Sultan. His famous words were that he wanted to die in Sultan.

I'd call to touch base; but had no interest speaking with me. Often he'd be feeling pretty woozy from the booze. Then in our short conversations, he'd pass the phone to Gisele. I'd hear him holler at her, to get him another beer! This without a doubt cut our conversation short. I always had the impression I was bothering him.

The last time I spoke with him he made it clear, his family was now Gisele and her kids. I was very patient, hoping he'd have a change of heart and his way of thinking; from then on, I'd just call only on special occasions.

Months following my breakup, I received a call in the middle of the night. It was my drunken father; he was slurring his words. He heard through the grapevine, I had separated. I wasn't too pleased to have been woken up by someone yelling at me, let alone someone drunk. He started to lecture me on why and how could I leave my husband? When we were married, Daniel was Dad's drinking buddy, whenever they were together.

I interrupted the conversation, made it clear it wasn't any of his business. That he wasn't the best example, saying if he didn't have anything better to say, I would hang up. He continued yelling and swearing at me. I told him this conversation was finished, I hung up. I didn't speak to him again for nearly twenty-two years. They would come to visit Gisele's children, once or twice a year; her children were sworn to secrecy.

I heard Gisele passed away; Jackie had kept contact with Dad; more so following her death.

Jackie called to inform me, Dad had been admitted to the hospital in Chapleau. He was in for high blood pressure and his diabetes. He was retaining water in his legs, and they were becoming purple and so swollen he could barely walk.

My two brothers didn't waste a minute leaving Quebec to go to his bedside. They spoke to Dad's doctor, who was totally against discharging him. Let alone doing a twelve-hour drive in thirty-plus weather with no air-conditioning; at 75 years old.

Though Dr. Taylor was Dad's physician for over thirty years; they fired him. They left the hospital with Dad. They stopped at his house, for clothing, medication, along with a few personal belongings.

They had him convinced; he was on his way for a two-week holiday at one of their homes. Emphasizing on how the specialists in Joliette were superior, compared to the ones in Sudbury. It was easy to trick him; he was on heavy duty medication. And very ill! They promised to get him up on his feet. This event is registered in the social worker's file at Joliette Hospital, including the Le Curateur Public du Quebec.

His stay, lasting over a year totally against his will. He was hospitalized a couple of times. When he was finally stabilized, the social workers had him transferred to a long-term facility in Joliette. Instead of listening to Dad's only wish to bring him back home. Dad refused to return to live with them! There was a tremendous amount of fighting and bickering between the siblings.

Laura came down for a holiday, the timing couldn't have been better. We received an unexpected call from a brother, stating there was a last minute family meeting at the hospital concerning Dad's health situation. We were both unaware of his situation, since it's been years we haven't had any contact with him.

We needed to explain to the head nurse, we wanted to visit Dad, and also prepare him for the next day's meeting. Dad had no clue there was a family meeting; let alone know it concerned him. Our brother tried to convince the nurse, we were there to cause trouble. She asked Dad, if he was comfortable with us visiting him, "yes, he replied, but he didn't want any problems." We had a short nice visit; our brother wouldn't give us our privacy. He was acting as Dad's bodyguard. We saw him from a distance, standing with his arms crossed; like a prison guard, not even speaking to him.

The meeting was to be held in a conference room at the hospital, by Dad's doctors, physiotherapist, psychologist and social worker. We were to figure out who was to take care of his belongings, estate, and where he was going to live next! Jackie came down to visit; together we tried to grant him his last wish; to bring him back home!,

Since the ten siblings, who were present at the meeting couldn't agree on some of the major decisions; the Public Trustee was assigned to take over Dad's file.

Once the meeting was terminated Laura and I continued on our road trip as planned to beautiful Quebec City.

On my return, I found out someone had been making withdrawals from Dad's bank account. Even though he was in the hospital! I went to the Public Trustee to file a complaint. They suggested I stop all actions in his accounts. That's exactly what I did.

There was also the question of selling his home. Of course he was totally against this, since he had built this home thirty years ago and was expecting to return home!

We worked with the most comprehensive and compassionate social worker—she was the best! She told him, if she had a magic wand, he would've been home by now. That would've been amazing!

My sister, Janette, her husband Roche and I would visit him every day. We eventually alternated the days. This was more convenient for me: I would leave the moment my day's work was done. It was between one hour to two hour drive; depending on the road conditions, one way. It seemed like I was the one who hit every blizzard, and ice storms, but it didn't stop me. I was committed!

On this gorgeous Saturday, when I exited the elevator, I noticed an older man sitting on a hard wooden chair at the end of the hall looking outside; the huge snowflakes were slowly coming down. The brothers managed to convince the doctor to have an ankle monitor put on him, so he couldn't leave the hospital floor.

My heart-ached when I saw his face, he had tears rolling down his cheeks. It was my father who was homesick; wanting to go back home— he was fed up of being there saying, living there was worse than being in prison.

I came bringing some exciting news to cheer him up. I spoke to the Trustee, about a week before Christmas. We came to an agreement, I could take Dad out for Christmas supper. When I told him my plan; we embraced and cried with joy.

The hospital and Trustee soon realized we weren't there to cause any trouble; contrary to what they were informed. They were more lenient on him. Finally the doctor insisted his ankle monitor be removed!

The truth was he was now an aging man, who wouldn't hurt a fly. I allowed myself to become acquainted with this old man. He wasn't the same father I knew; we had a nice connection!

We discussed the pass, which was very emotional for us both. He was remorseful for what he did; asking for forgiveness for the hurt he caused.

I read Laura's letter she wrote him; he was touched—he couldn't hold back the tears. He was deeply regretful that he had caused so much pain; again asking for her pardoning as well!

He was very appreciative of everything Janette and Roche did for him; expressing how Roche was more like a son then his own.

Laura and Jackie called regularly on Dad's cell. Jackie had purchased it for him; since they lived out of the province. This made it easier for us to keep in contact; encouraging him to not give up. He was free to call whomever, without walking to the nurse's desk.

We supported, and did our best to keep him thinking positively; repeating we are doing everything within our powers to get him home.

We made the best of our time together. We'd bring him fruits, yogurt and cakes along with anything he desired. I bought him a watch since his was stolen, at the residence with a pair of runners; his were falling apart.

I even attempted to make beet soup, known as borscht; a Ukrainian dish. Dad had the desire for this meal now for the past few weeks. Ironically, it turned out pretty darn tasty; above all he was proud of me! I made an effort to spoil him; that's just who I am! Forgiving him helped us to rebuild our father and daughter relationship. I was totally accepting of my new father!

The social worker and the Public Trustee came to a conclusion; to have him transferred to Sudbury. This was overly exciting news to us. We could finally have peace of mind—he was at last going home! At the same time, I was feeling heartbroken; grieving the loss of the father I've always dreamed of.

Jackie drove down to bring him to his temporary residence. Dad was hopeful as well as incredibly pleased; being one step away from home.

He had received a call through the residence, which startled him. He immediately called Jackie and me to share how he was feeling. We both expressed how immensely proud of him we were; considering the conversation.

Jackie requested he get prepared, she was on her way. They went to feed the ducks at the pond outside of the hospital. When Jackie explained what happened next; she broke down and was speechless.

While they were feeding the ducks; she was having a conversation with him. She couldn't understand a word he was saying. He was mumbling, she told him to stop fooling around, since he liked to pull pranks on people. All of a sudden she realized his face was droopy, she panicked with adrenaline, she put him in the truck; brought him straight to the ER. The doctor's diagnosis wasn't good; he has suffered a massive stroke!

I felt the urge to rush to his bedside; I spent a week and a half with Jackie. Three or four days later, he suffered from another. This one was the end! Now, he was hooked up to every existing life support machine. It looked as though he recognized me, but my name was indistinct.

We said our farewells; I pronounced those famous words, "I love you and it's ok to let go." Letting him know how grateful I was to have reconnected after all of this time; I'd see him in another world. Obviously, it was clear to see he was stuck in his own body; as one tear rolled down his face. It was a very emotional and heartbreaking moment. Jackie and I did our share of crying!

His condition had stabilized, but the diagnosis wasn't promising. It was essential I return to my career. The doctors couldn't predict the exact time frame of death. I left Sudbury on October 30th.

On my return I had a shift in the ER. There was this elderly man needing to be rushed to the ICU. As I was racing through the hallways; those silent tears suddenly resurfaced. I found it difficult focusing on where I was heading. I tried calming my emotions, and thinking to myself;

the old man wasn't Dad. I lost my self-control; I could not manage to get a grip. I requested a time-out!

It suddenly hit me like a brick wall; this is exactly how my father died; hooked up to all kinds of machines being rushed to intensive care just to pass away. May you rest-in-peace!

I was also feeling guilty! I couldn't hold his hand, to comfort him and reassure him; telling him I loved him for the last time. For the superstitious, Friday the 13th is bad luck, but for him it was his lucky day. His suffering ended on Friday, December 13, 2013.

Chapter seventeen

I had been in contact with Dave Koski for the past few years. He tracked me down on social media after we lost touch a few years ago. This is exactly how our first conversation went on Messenger in December 2013. "Hi, I'm Dave Kaski and I'm wondering if you are the Anne-Marie I knew in Sudbury. If so, I would like to know how you are doing. Thanks!"

I replied, "Hello...I just want to say I don't think I'm the person you're looking for. I don't think I know you???" He was using another person's Facebook account.

He responded, "Thank you for your reply. The Anne-Marie I knew lived on Santala Road near Lively. She also had sisters named Laura, Jackie, Margaret and a brother Paul last name used to be Mac Donald and another brother living in Sudbury. I used to spell my name Dave Koski, but it is now Kaski. If you're not that Anne-Marie sorry to have bothered you Thanks!"

At first I told myself *yeah right, what's the chance of him being my Dave?* But, when he wrote back I honestly couldn't believe his message that we've reconnected once again. I jumped for joy with my two arms in the air, repeating *OMG!! Is this for real?* I had tears of joy. It was such an emotional moment. Everyone was happy and excited for me, I was on cloud nine!

He pointed out; he had tried to reach me around 1992 or 1993, saying a girl picked up the phone. In that moment I had a flash of Annie giving me the message; saying an English-speaking man had called and wanted me to return his call. There was just a slight problem with that—we didn't have a caller ID and Annie didn't write his name or phone number down.

When I pressed charges against Bernie, I remember calling Helen to get his number. I wanted to know if he would support the process of getting a paternity test, if required. He said he would without any hesitation. I was kind of surprised to hear that. To my knowledge, Jehovah Witnesses don't do blood work. But again, what do I know about this religion?

He had eventually moved on and changed numbers; lost mine during his move.

He couldn't remember the city I lived in. Still no internet! I had lots on my plate with the court case; taking care of my children. I just brushed it off saying, if it was important he'll call back.

When I'd return for a visit to Sudbury, I'd often make time to visit his mom; always asking about Dave. Love for him ran in my veins!

It seemed like, every time I was single he wasn't; when he was I wasn't. The truth of the matter is we've been following one another, since our youthful years.

In 2016 he was unhappily married. Things started to get serious between us; we'd communicated over the phone and the internet. All we could think about was how amazing it would be to be in each other's arms, one more time…Our relationship escalated rapidly, until we were speaking to each other every spare moment we had. You can't imagine how exciting and alive I felt—this was definitely a long time coming.

He mentioned that he'd come to visit; expressing his strong desire to see me. He said on his way he'd make a stop in Kingston for the night. That didn't happen, I'm assuming he was impatient and wanted to get here sooner than later.

We met on my evening break at the hospital. I was glowing when I returned to work. I was one hyper nurse's aide going a little crazy! Can you blame me? I was in love again! Everyone was happy for me. I was laughing, crying and jumping for joy!

After my evening shift, we headed to the Super 8 Hotel, where I had made reservations on the spot. We had a spa in the room. We didn't have time to use it; we'd need to keep it for future use.

He came on February 17, 2017. His birthday was on the 18th believe me, it was a birthday he will never forget; neither will I for that matter!

Everyone expressed, "He must really love you, to come 465 miles just to see you." Yes he does, and the feeling's totally mutual!

We were drinking wine and beer, relaxing on the loveseat, soaking up every precious moment. As we gazed into each other's eyes, I could barely grasp the fact; he was sitting next to me, while rubbing my feet with his tender touch. After hours of talking and getting cozy with each other, I jumped in the shower. We chatted again for a long time—our passion for each other was growing by the minute. Our feelings were as strong as ever! Every time we've reconnected it seems like only yesterday, although yesterday took part of us away. Tomorrow was what we were waiting for. Our feelings for each other hadn't changed over the years.

> The heart never forgets the things that made it feel so light.
> It keeps in loving memory the things so warm and bright.
> The words of real encouragement that kept it from despair!
> The little deeds of thoughtfulness that softly say I care.
> The heart does not forget such things.
> I know that this is true.
> My heart is filled with many special thoughts.
> My one and only love!

Honestly it took a small adjustment to get used to my hunk of a man going bald! He remained my love, my one and only beloved. This affection could never die! We embraced one another; we continued being intimate into the wee hours of the night. I'd wake up often keeping my body touching him. This absolutely felt surreal; it was so perfect to be in his arms where I should be!

Due to the ending of his marriage, he was disfellowshipped from his congregation; shunned by Jehovah's Witnesses. These people call themselves family!

He was now a free agent to visit whenever we desired. There was no one to control our every move, or thought. We were together; we enjoyed being dependent on each other as a couple. I had no problem with it. I thought, doesn't this feel amazing? Also isn't it exactly what God wants for all of his children? God wants his family to be happy without judgment, and to love one another as one huge family. Isn't that why he created us? Dave was free to feel his true feelings, doing everything his heart desired including being with me; the person he had always loved!

We'd Skype for hours a day, before my work on my breaks, supper breaks and after work. There were times I saw him pinch himself to check, if he wasn't dreaming I'd say," Nope! This is real Babe, and I'm not going anywhere!" We couldn't get enough of each other. It was unbelievable how we always had something new to say. He was always curious if I had heard anything about Christine. He told me he had suffered from a depression, while being in a very dark place after we broke up. The moment he mentioned that I had a flash of Gram filling me in with how sick he was and going through an extremely hard time. Gram and I kept contact by phone and letters, until she passed away.

Dave was now pensioned; he was free as a bird; nothing stopping him now!

It was my honour to have him return in May. I had booked my hospital holidays to go visit his mom and sibling, whom I hadn't seen in years. Everyone was delighted to see me. Honestly, his mother and his kids especially, were praying for his freedom; not return to being a Jehovah's Witnesses!

It's amazing how cruel love can be. No one else can understand what it means to have been through it all just to fall into a sea of darkness. No one can understand, what it means to land so close to the edge. It was amazing to be back in that home. So many awesome memories have been made here.

Of course his mother also questioned if I had any news, or the whereabouts of Christine. The only information I could give her was she was at the army base in Quebec City.

We stayed for a couple of days, and headed down to southern Ontario where he lived. His daughter Sonia had heard about me over the years. He told her about us having a baby together. She resided about fifteen minutes from him. We had an amazing visit; it seemed like we've known each other forever. We had a common interest—it was to see Dave happy. We thought it would've been sweet to extend our families. She would have loved for me to be her stepmother; so would have I.

Sonia and her fiancé Adam gave me an invitation to go to their wedding on July 8th, 2017. They were unaware; Dave had already asked me to be his date. Such an honour! I wouldn't have missed this most important celebration for anything.

Taking the plane was fast, but I couldn't arrive fast enough—first the flight; then a two-hour drive, but who was counting?

We welcomed his siblings with a wedding breakfast, on the morning of the wedding. Everything was made with love. It was amazing to see everyone together; it felt like home!

Some said it was their first time entering his place. But, now the circumstances were perfect. The wedding was amazing and magical, not to mention it was the most precious time ever. Sonia and Adam I will forever cherish your love, kindness and generosity. You are in my heart forever!

The weather was perfect, a bit on the chilly side, but I had Dave to keep me warm. Everyone was so compassionate and very accepting of us. I walked with my head high, I felt proud—I was Dave's lady. I told Dave and others that our love story was the best!

Shortly after being back to work on a few evening shifts, I found it necessary to consult at the emergency room. I was experiencing extreme fatigue for a few months.

Dave was very concerned! We made an agreement; I'd call on my cell phone, every evening when I'd finish my shift. This way he could keep me concentrated on our conversation, so I wouldn't fall asleep driving—that's how terrible it was. I was exhausted; it definitely was worse following my shift, I wasn't sure I'd make it home safe. I had already experienced this kind of extreme fatigue when I was diagnosed with thyroid cancer.

This time I was in stage-three kidney disease. My GFR test results were abnormal; my kidneys were functioning at forty-seven percent. I was now forced onto sick leave.

I'd often try to look-up Christine. With the hope she had opened a Facebook account. The problem was, there were too many people with the same name. Over the years, I called numbers thinking it might be her. Some responded; no such person, or simply had the wrong number; others would just slam the phone down in my ear.

One night around 1a.m. a post popped up onto my Facebook page; for free Canada Adoption/ Family Search. I made a request to join this group; I immediately was accepted, considering the amount of information I furnished. I gave the names of the adopted aunts, uncles, adopted father's name, where they were living at the time of adoption, where they moved once Mom bought their house and the baby's birth date and date of adoption. What threw us off track for a short period of time; one Christine had two young children, but weren't living on the army base.

We continued our search; kept our faith we'd find her sooner than later. I gave a call to this one lady who was confused about what I wanted. They were not pleased. Obviously, it wasn't her. Through our investigation we believe this lady was Christine's cousin, Leona and Ron's daughter.

I took a chance on sending messages to Christine and her husband who had two young children. I wrote on two separate Messenger accounts. I asked if his wife was adopted, he replied. "Yes." Wow! Out of all the possible Christine's we found her! Her husband and I exchanged the names of the adopted family. She was remarried, had two more children and was no longer living on the military base in Quebec.

Turns out Leona and Ron were Christine's godparents. We exchanged a few pictures of our kids, siblings and the pictures from her day of adoption. Her husband didn't hold back indicating how much Christine resembled Gram; which she definitely did. Some have also indicated how she bears a resemblance to one of Dave's brothers. Helen without hesitation said she looked just like her mother! One also said she resembled my mother.

Even though there was never a positive DNA test to prove paternity. I am convinced she's Dave's daughter, he also was incredibly pleased.

I did try an Ancestry DNA test. I paid for a couple of months, but I didn't feel like I was getting anywhere. I couldn't believe how the timing was so perfect for Free Adoption Canada.

On February 8th, 2018, at 5:32 a.m. there was a post to the Facebook group. The administrator in Kingsville Ontario wrote:

"Anne-Marie Courtemanche's daughter has been found! After many messages and cold calling to several people, our dedication and persistence paid off.

Thanks, Anne-Marie for your patience and trust in me! Keep the faith!

This is the new beginning to the rest of your life!!!"

Christine's husband told me she wasn't ready to meet or speak with me at this point in time. Most importantly I know she is healthy and happy. This was important for me; it had been a constant concern of mine over the years. This was a great relief. It clearly took some worry and weight off of my shoulders. For sure it couldn't have been easier for her either, to have her biological mother to all of a sudden appear into her life.

I heard the Ed Sheeran love song "Perfect" on the radio in August 2017 with perfect timing. It honestly represents our life and our love story. I have friends saying when they hear it they automatically think of us. I felt it was the most appropriate love song to include in my autobiography. I can guarantee the next time you hear it you will automatically think of us. https://www.youtube.com/watch?v=UDDMYw_IZnE

After spending a week together, it was time for me to leave again. I was over the moon, how far and fast our relationship had spiraled. We were content! I absolutely knew we were heading in the right direction in our lives. I was single now for thirteen years. Everyone found it very special that my very first boyfriend had returned into my life. We had the most remarkable memories together; we both wanted to spend our lives together.

In July he asked me to marry him. I told him I would in a heartbeat, except for the fact I couldn't be a Jehovah's Witness.

I expressed how it could function, if we respected each other's faith; there are many inter-religious couples. We cried in each other's arms, once more.

The motorcycle rides were the best, feeling so free! It was wonderful to have my arms around him once again; with his tender touch stroking my thigh, while riding around town. I fell deeply in love! These were the best times ever! I truly felt important and proud to be his girl once again! He was anxious to introduce me to his friends. You could see how proud he was, to bring me out to the Jazz Bar where at times he would host the evening jam. He is a fine musician!

Around the middle of August 2017, he called explaining why we couldn't continue to see each other anymore. This was like a knife stab through the heart. It was devastating! I honestly felt like he had ripped my heart out of my chest. He may as well have shot me dead! I couldn't understand—we had so much pleasure together. Our family and friends were excited and thrilled to finally see us happy together. But Why!

It was unbelievable how much I cried, when he told me he needed to break up. Believe it or not, I wept for months. I couldn't believe he was doing this to me; most importantly to us, after everything we'd been through. After many years being separated it still hurts; I still get choked up thinking, or talking about us. This was something I had feared once I'd leave to come home.

He mentioned he wanted to be reinstated at the Kingdom Hall of Jehovah's Witnesses. I couldn't believe he would sacrifice his happiness for a man-made religion, from New York!

What? God doesn't want his people happy.

Many expressed how he had changed for the better, when we were dating; becoming happier and less of a grouch. They hadn't seen him that happy in many years. He expressed how he felt alive; I made him feel like a man again!

I had no choice in the matter, since I lived so far away to try to do anything about the situation. We do speak once and a while to see how the other is doing. He always seems so happy. He's so easy to keep a conversation with. He decided it would be best for him to end our video chats; he clearly stated I was too tempting for him!

His mother fell ill, but she is a trooper. I visited her in October 2018. Dave also was visiting with Sonia and his granddaughter. I stayed at his sister Helga and her husband Phil's. Sonia called at Helga's, saying Dave was in agreement, I met his four-month-old granddaughter Lila. She is his only grandchild. She's just adorable!

I was honoured to be able to meet her as a baby. I genuinely enjoyed my visit with them all, once again. Everyone noticed how Dave and I couldn't keep our eyes off of each other. It's in times like this we need to have self-respect, along with self-control! I believe the hurt was deep, because our love was genuine. It's been said that everyone will find true love once in their existence and I believe he is mine!

> I don't think he will ever know how much love I have to give,
> I wonder if he even knows he is the reason why I live?
> I'd change my orbit to banish his night

Just to keep him in my nurturing light.
Our fates intertwined two bodies in motion.
Through time and space our dance of devotion!
If he was an island I'd be his sea.
Caressing his shores soft and gentle as can be!
My tidal embrace would leave gifts on his sands,
With my currents and storms I'd wash his gentle lands.

Unfortunately, that was the last time I saw him.

His sister Helga and I have an incredibly special friendship—we chat mainly on Messenger and on video chat. She keeps me updated on Helen's situation, along with the rest of the family. She is the mini portrait of Gram. Sonia and I also keep in touch; she's such a caring companionate human being!

Chapter eighteen

ADDITIONAL INFORMATION

Now, for my kidneys! Everything seems to be good. My filtration rate (GFR) is stable at sixty. For now we are keeping a close eye on it via blood tests. According to the National Kidney Foundation, the normal range is between ninety to a hundred and twenty. Now it's just something else to worry about. When is it too much for one person to handle?

The doctor assumes my kidney problems came from taking Arthrotec, a non-steroidal anti-inflammatory drug (NSAID) I've been taken-twice daily for six years for treating my osteoarthritis. He insisted I cease the medication.

After just a few days, I felt the horrible effect of following his directions. It took every part of me to get out of bed, as the pain was so unbearable. I quickly called my family doctor who tried me on morphine, Opioid and different prescriptions, but nothing seemed to relieve any pain.

I finally asked to see our staff hospital's doctor. He clearly stated I was unable to return to the hospital to work and ordered an MRI. I paid $685.00 at a private clinic to try to advance the waiting time otherwise; at the hospital I wouldn't have had an appointment before six months to a year.

I was just so sore; fed up with the waiting game; waiting almost two months in between each appointment.

After my MRI at least I knew where I stood. I had multiple hernias, with anterior displacement of a vertebra 7.5mm relative to the one below. My spine had started to slip, due to degenerative disc disease, and I had a couple of bulging discs with a couple of small spinal stenosis. I had to avoid extended walking, lifting and sitting for a long amount of time. I am now patiently waiting to consult a Neurosurgeon.

My doctor mentioned, possibly putting a metal plate, fusing some vertebrae, and the shaving of a couple of bulging hernias.

In October 2018, the doctor's secretary said, I'd most likely consult with a neurosurgeon only in 2019. I asked if Hawkesbury Hospital in Ontario would be covered with the Quebec medical card. Yes, she replied, and thought it was an awesome idea. Since this was out of province, she mentioned it would probably be faster. I quickly contacted the hospital; then faxed the paperwork.

Sure enough, I received a call within nine days with dates for an EMG test and an appointment to see a neurologist on May 17th, 2019 to get the results from my tests and my diagnosis. I was then put on a waiting list for the best care for my situation. Obviously, I was in the wrong province. Why didn't we think of that before?

I just want my back problems to be more tolerable. As of this moment, I'm taking; Tramadol an Opioid analgesic, with six Tylenol Arthritis daily. It seems to help somewhat. Taking so much Tylenol will be hard on my liver; if it's not one thing it's another. I just can't wait to be free of the extreme pain, and the medications. I'm anxious to have to return to some kind of normalcy.

I did finally receive a call from McGill Hospital. Dr. Benoit Goulet in October 2020 told me he was ready to do my spinal fusion surgery. I refused, I wasn't ready just yet. I also explained, I started a new job at the hospital, as a security agent at the triage; for the COVID 19. He suggested I contact him when I'm ready. As for right now, I'm not doing any strenuous activities; no need to be on any medication.

I've come to a point in my life, where I cannot deny the many issues and losses I had suffered due to childhood abuse; the mental and physical pain, abandonment, the loss of my childhood, my innocence, siblings, future and mostly the loss of my firstborn.

I refused to think about the details of those days, as it made me feel depressed, and I wanted to isolate myself from everyone. My mind and memories had suffocated the air I breathed. There were many times

I wanted to sleep my life away, but I fought, I fought hard to save my inner child.

Laura contacted Susan, our crown attorney in June 2014. She still remembers us after all those years. She said that she was just beginning her career when she met us, but up to this day; twenty-one years later our case was still the worst case of sexual abuse she'd ever encountered. This was great to hear to a certain degree. It confirmed how horrible our lives were.

In 2017-2018 I signed myself up to go to group therapy for a sixteen weeks program, at CALACS des Laurentides. This is an organization that offers psychosocial aid and support to victims of sexual abuse.

This is the only help that seriously relieved my pain and suffering. With my story, I did make a few people in the group cry. We were ten women, fighting to free ourselves from the hell that was forced upon us.

I'm thankful to Dave for the encouragement. He explained to me how I could benefit from the therapy in many ways. He was perfectly right! It was an unexpectedly positive experience for me indeed. There are certain situations that will resurface, but we were taught how to cope with the emotional pain; if they would resurface.

In the group I volunteered to share my story first—I just wanted to get it over with. As I told my story, some of these broken women felt like theirs were nothing compared to mine. Some others felt they weren't strong enough to tell their stories openly to strangers. I told them, though my story might not be the same as theirs, I believed the pain remains the same. A few ladies broke down crying, as I shared my story. They truly felt my hurt!

I now believe my purpose in life is to write a book that will help the countless victims become survivors.

I wrote to Celine Dion in June 1998 to see if she was interested in making another movie. She had already made an extremely popular mini-series in French about the child-abuse of Elisa Trudel. Its title is Des Fleurs Sur a Neige. Celine was an excellent actress; she played the victim.

I received a letter from her producers, including the summarization I had sent of my story. They sent their best regards, and were very compassionate and sympathetic. They encouraged me to lean towards other actors, or production companies; she wasn't going to be making another movie on child abuse.

I also contacted the *Dini* CTV Talk Show in Toronto, on February 16, 1999 to see if I could go on the show. The reply from CTV Toronto stated, the show was soon to be cancelled.

While going through our trial I was approached to appear on the *Sally* TV Talk Show in Toronto. I was honoured, but I needed to turn them down. Due to the fact that I didn't think I was psychologically ready to tell the world just yet, as I was still dealing with the court case.

I was hoping Christine had stored her DNA in the database. I also wrote to Freedom of Information and Protection of Privacy in June 2017 to try to get access from the DNA database files. Since the courts knew where she was, I was hoping that records of this were being held by the Crown Law Office and the Criminal Law Division, or the Ministry of the Attorney General. The answer came back negative.

The judge had ordered Bernie and me to put our DNA in the National Database for future possible use. Bernie was resistant, but had a court order. Isn't it ironic how suddenly he felt threatened? He should've been horror-struck long before this.

Laura wrote to Dr. Phil and she received a response—he was willing to see us. But, Laura realized she wasn't quite ready at this time in her life. She suggested I go on my own. She would forward me the correspondence and the complete file; I categorically said, "No! We are a team." So of course it was a no-go!

I wrote Christine a letter trying to explain the situation from my point of view; received no response. I touched base again on December 3rd, 2018 asking if she had taken the time to read my letter and asking her to try to consider where I was coming from; especially since she was now a mother. I do my best to stay positive in hopes that she'll eventually come around. I just can't wait till we meet again!

I've always had a hard time watching TV in comfort. I'd be watching movies with tight fists and the moment I would see a naked woman, or even a half-naked woman, I'd jump up in rage and go to another room. If I were with someone else, they'd tell me to calm down. I had no control over my reactions; it wasn't pleasant for anyone around me. I would also be mad at myself for reacting in certain ways. Some have just come straight out and told me I had a mental problem.

While living through the heat of summer I've always tried my best to choose the day to run my errands. Girls are half-dressed in shopping centers on the sidewalks; this has caused an enormous amount of stress. I'd many times end up with a debilitating migraine headache; become bedridden for a week or longer. It was not pleasant for my kids to see me in so much pain; paralyzed in my bed.

I've always been self-conscious on what to wear leaving my home. I never wanted to draw any unwanted attention to myself.

My sex life could be better I am sure, ha-ha! It is far from my priority right now. There were times when I was living with my husband or a spouse; they'd touch me in a certain way, which would remind me of Bernie. Instant flashback!

When guys in general show any affection, I think they just want me for sex. This made it hard to comprehend the difference between ordinary friendship, or sexual attraction?

For me sex was, make it fast; get it over with! I felt it was dirty and disgusting for so many years. There were times when I'd have flashbacks and felt like a prostitute feeling filthy; then felt the need to shower!

Trusting men and saying no never came easy. I'm proud of how I've overcome a lot of these unwanted reactions. I'm still learning to control and calm my emotions. I'm definitely no longer the person I was, thank God!

Throughout my life, I have often wondered what it would be like to be a guy. It took me many years to accept my woman's body and gain my self-confidence.

There were many days I'd be emotionally beat, while breaking down crying stating "I wish I could've had a normal life." The question of the matter is what was normal?

I learned at the ripe young age of seven, to hide my feelings through laughter, teasing, pretending everything was fine and dandy. Today my mask needs to come off, and stay off. My hurt is deep. This is me—the true me.

In raising my two boys I didn't have any major problems. They did what the average teenage boys did. I raised them to have respect for girls. To never, ever, lay a hand on one; neither with force or in any other way a girl would feel uncomfortable.

Annie was a whole different story. I over-protected her; she said it was very hurtful, and too much for a little girl to bear.

For example when she started her menstrual cycle at nine years old, I freaked out. I had been the assigned person to be the teacher for my siblings, but everyone had been over the age of eleven.

I sat her down and said, "Do not ever let a boy touch your private parts." I was getting very worked up, having to talk about this! She was so young and I didn't want her to suffer in any way. There had already been times, she'd come in crying saying the guys said she wasn't good enough for them; she didn't want to kiss them.

I continued talking to her, as I explained, "If a guy wants to do bad things to you or something you're not comfortable with you show them your hand, and say go do your own job."

I let her know she could come to me, or at least speak to another adult. I made it clear, I was always here, if she ever needed to talk.

I am finding kids are engaging in sexual activities younger and younger these days. Which I'm sure will freak out many other parents.

I feel so terribly embarrassed, now that I did this to my baby girl. Why and how? After all this time I believe I reacted out of fear, to protect my little princess. She was maturing too quickly, and I wasn't ready, or pre-pared. I can't express enough the regret and the guilt I have for saying those things to her.

Thank goodness she's an incredible young lady, who has made me proud with her achievements and gave me two gorgeous granddaughters. She is doing an awesome job of raising them. She has found the perfect father for her children!

She wrote in so many birthdays, Christmas and Mother's Day cards that she was sorry for everything she'd done wrong. But, she hadn't done any wrong; she was just being a normal young teenager reacting to an overprotective mother.

I was that freaked-out country girl that moved to the city. I was terribly scared for her. Scared she'd get hurt by the boys. Afraid I wouldn't be there to protect her, if ever she needed protection. Unfortunately, I overreacted in every way to her, I'm so deeply sorry—I did the best I could with what I had to work with.

Raising kids hadn't been taught to me. I was dealing with everyday child problems as they arose. But, as I know today, I didn't handle it in the best way.

Yes, I have acknowledged Annie suffered from my strictness. For me, I saved her from sexually and psychological abuse. Most importantly she was free from a lifetime of pain and guilt.

Thank goodness I've grown; I have more self-respect and a whole new perspective on life. It's been a long bumpy road, but I believe I'm back on track to where I was meant to be. Today I'm blessed to have three awesome adult children.

Bernie's behaviour had an enormous impact and caused permanent damage to us all. I'm at a point where I'm doing my best to turn that negativity into making the best of each day, while remaining positive. I am still confident that one day Prince Charming will sweep me off my feet, and I'll have a fairytale wedding and live happily ever after!

Today I look back at my life's journey, and ask myself, "was that even humanly possible?" I am a proud survivor! I've been to hell and back a few times.

After I told parts of my story to Laura's doctor in Wetaskiwin Alberta, his immediate response was, "And you didn't kill yourself? " That really hit home for me. This was in 2010. It made me realize even more, how far I had come in this world.

That amazing caring man Doctor Schlenther had been treating Laura for her post-traumatic stress disorder. She was blessed to have such a compassionate and understanding doctor, who supported and saw her through her healing. He truly went out of his way, to get her the best medical help possible.

I pray our story will persuade other abused victims to come out of the closet and face their abusers head-on. Yes, it wasn't always easy, but you're never alone. You'd be surprised by your support group, family, friends, kids, husbands and even complete strangers.

Facing your abuser will generate closure, on the not-so-bright spots of your personal history and create emotional and psychological healing. I genuinely want other victims to be encouraged, to break their silence and experience how therapeutic this can be.

#ME TOO MOVEMENT; one by one
we'll get there
self-confidence—self-respect—self-love—love to help others.

Together we are one. You're stronger than you think.

I've always wondered why God would let such abuses happen to me and other children: As they say, there's a reason for everything.

Ecclesiastes 3 King James Version (KJV)

To everything there is a season and a time for every purpose
under heaven:
A time to be born and a time to die; a time to plant and a time to pluck
up that which is planted;
A time to kill and a time to heal; a time to break down and a time to
build up;
A time to weep and a time to laugh; a time to mourn and a time
to dance;
A time to cast away stones and a time to gather stones together; a time to
embrace and a time to refrain from embracing;
A time to get and a time to lose; a time to keep and a time to cast away;
A time to rend and a time to sew; a time to keep silent and a time
to speak;
A time to love and a time to hate; a time of war and a time of peace.

What profit hath he that worketh in that wherein he laboureth?
I have seen the travail, which God hath given to the sons of men to be
exercised in it.
He hath made everything beautiful in his time: also he hath set the world
in their heart so that no man can find out the work that God maketh
from the beginning to the end.
I know that there is no good in them, but for a man to rejoice and to do

well in his life.
And also that every man should eat and drink and enjoy the good of all
his labour, it is the gift of God.
I know that whatsoever God doeth, it shall be forever: nothing can be put
to it, nor anything was taken from it: and God doeth it, that men should
fear before him.
That which hath been is now; and that which is to be hath already been;
and God requireth that which is past.
And moreover, I saw under the sun the place of judgment, that wicked-
ness was there; and the place of righteousness, that iniquity was there.
I said in mine heart God shall judge the righteous and the wicked: for
there is a time for every purpose and for every work.
I said in my heart concerning the estate of the sons of men that God
might manifest them and that they might see that they themselves
are beasts.
For that which befalleth the sons of men befalleth beasts; even one thing
befalleth them: as the one dieth so dieth the other; yea, they have all one
breath; so that a man hath no preeminence above a beast: for all is vanity.
All go unto one place; all are of the dust and all turn to dust again.
Who knoweth the spirit of man that goeth upward and the spirit of the
beast that goeth downward to the earth?
Wherefore I perceive that there is nothing better than that a man should
rejoice in his own works; for that is his portion: for who shall bring him
to see what shall be after him?

It's just today I can rejoice in this Bible verse. It helped me to raise my three awesome children and made me a stronger woman.

Today I can help other victims, through their hard times, by talking and writing and possibly this could lead up to producing a movie, as I've also dreamed of!

As children, Laura and I attended mass many times a week. Serving helped us keep our sanity. Through all the abuses sexual, physical and mental we learned to trust in Jesus.

Due to all the events of life that were thrown at us we learned to depend upon God's word. God has proven time and time again that he will be there for us. He saw how our hearts were broken in two, but he found a way to fix them for us.

As we look back at where we have been, and how far we have come and we see that he is still God and he was fighting for us all along.

He will do it for you too! He will always come through for you. You may not know how. You may not know when, but He will do it for you.

I am proof that Satan is a liar! He tried to deceive me by saying that my troubles will never go away. He thought he had me bound, but Jesus set me free.

While we were on our knees pleading to the lovely lady dressed in blue Jesus touched us!

We felt we had no solution to our problems, but we found the answer while we were serving others. Jesus gave it to us. He set us free.

So, my friends, if you are confused, lost, abused, or scared don't despair God is not the police. He sees it all. I know that you can stand. Don't worry, because your life is in God's hands.

If your heart is broken, just know that no matter what may come your way, joy comes in the morning. Troubles don't last all day.

Look at me. I am standing proud and free! He'll do the same for you.

Huguette's birthday back left Anne-Marie Hector Courtemanche, Laura Huguette Dicaire with siblings Denis Sylvie Janette Lynn Johanne Frank and Josee Courtemanche, along with Huguette's next of kin. May 17, 1975.

Anne-Marie left (17) Huguette Dicaire
Dad and Laura (16)
St. Lin Ville des Laurentides.

Sally S. Matthews

In Loving Memory
of
Sally S. Matthews
39 Years

Tuesday afternoon, June 24th, 1980 at the Sudbury Memorial Hospital.

Beloved mother of Paul MacDonald, David MacDonald, John Courtemanche, Mary MacDonald, and Margaret Mac-Donald, all of Val Caron, Jacqueline Courtemanche of Sudbury, Mrs. Dan (Anne-Marie) Richard of Montreal and Mrs. Dan (Laura) Landry of Thunder Bay. Loving daughter of John Matthews of Thunder Bay and the late Vicky (predeceased). Dear grandmother of two grandchildren.

Resting at the

Lougheed Funeral Home
252 Regent St. S. at Hazel St.
Funeral Mass
in
Christ the King Church
Saturday, June 28th, 1980
at 10 a.m.
Rev. Fr. R. J. van Berkel officiating
Interment in the Valley East Cemetery

169

1st picture together Hector and me. Ste Lin Quebec May 1975.

Sally (36) Grampa John, Val Caron,
District of Sudbury 1976.

A week after my 19th birthday; back David Mac Donald Daniel Richard (left) Sally Anne-Marie. Taken in the famous driveway, where I took the last picture with Christine Lynn and signed the adoption paper. July 1976.

*Anne-Marie Richard (19) Daniel Richard (28)
Ste Lin Quebec March 12, 1977.*

1st operation for thyroidectomy; St. Jerome Hospital Spouse Stephane Brun Junior back middle Joey me and Annie; my favourite support team always! October 2006.

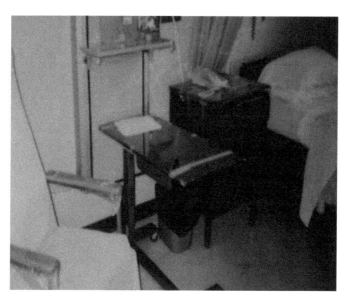

St. Luc Hospital, Montreal for Isotope Radiotherapy, I had three treatments over the next three years. Everything was covered and taped with plastic because I was radioactive. The bathroom floor was also covered and taped with plastic and soaker pads. January 2007.

Radioactive Iodine 131, Isotope Therapy.
St Luc Hospital Montreal January 2007.

Anne-Marie, Laura on right. 1st Christmas together in 38 years was also our last Camrose Alberta 2010.

Department of Lafontaine Long-term care
Anne-Marie back right Lachute Hospital September 2016.

Jackie Courtemanche; Taken at The Honourable James Jerome Sports Complex Sudbury, where Hector Joseph Courtemanche had his major stroke (Hospital seen in back) June 23, 2019.

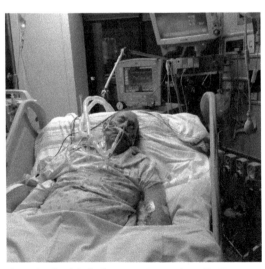

Hector Courtemanche on his death bed after a massive stroke in Sudbury, passed away December 13, 2013.

Sonia Koski and Adam Smart wedding, it was an honour to attend. How could I refuse!

July 8, 2017.

Anne-Marie Dave Koski at Jazzmyn's Open Mic. July 2017.

My pride and joy; Left Annie spouse Martin Demers Joey
Anne–Marie Junior left Kelly–Ann (6) Amy (4)
Fred and Helen' wedding 15, July 2017.

My three kids I am so proud of;
Junior Richard and Ari Kim' wedding Quebec September 30, 2017.

177

Joey Richard, spouse
Shar Simms from Alberta July 2018.

Annie Richard, spouse Martin Demers
Kelly-Ann Demers (7) Amy Demers (5) Feb 2018.

My Broken Soul

I think I know why you became my stepfather.
So you could take advantage of me, I gather!
I never said or gave you the right.
To bring me into your bed that night!

Mom pushed me towards you all the time.
That doesn't forgive her but, you're just slime!
Mom went to the hospital to have your child.
That was no excuse for you to go wild!

I didn't ask you to feel or touch me.
It happened every week, couldn't you see?
I didn't want to be your wife at fourteen.
I wanted normal love like any human being!

You robbed my life from seven to sixteen.
You bastard, you don't deserve to be seen!
When I got pregnant you put me in a shell.
Giving up my baby was sure living hell!

Thanks to you I'm not that strong.
I hope you rot in hell when you are gone!
When you took us in you must have had pity.
I can assure you my life is mighty shitty!

Today I'm not that strong, I know I have to fight.
Now, I can take you to court—I have the right!
You've had control all of my life up to now.
I'll show you control, I'll show you how!

Seeing your face in court again!
Just made me sick to feel my pain!

I must face my abuser, I know.
For myself to be able to live and grow!

If only I could start all over.
I wouldn't be in denial. I'd surely turn you over!
If there's any justice, I will gain.
After all this, I hope I'll have less pain!

-By Anne-Marie Courtemanche
Written March 6, 1995

Afterword

Sally Matthews, I will never comprehend how, or why you would betray your own children. You were very selfish. What the hell were you thinking? You left me alone with a monster in those dark desperate years. You've now left this life and to no surprise you have left me with so many unanswered questions. How and why would a mother let her children be tortured in any way whatsoever? It must have seemed just so easy to turn a blind eye. Why the hell did you have kids?

Additional Information

Worker: O.W. Girdlestone/lv
Date: Aug. 30th, 1972.

Aug. 24th, 1972 - Notes.

MacDonald -Loy Wellington Street, Phone 692-9335, Creighton, Ontario.
(Oakland Bank).

In reading the file it seems that this family moved out of our care in April or May of 1966. At the time we had been of some service. Mr. Bernie Dumont, lawyer, was handling the matter of custody. The CKIB had been asked to help with spectacles for John, age 9. Today we received a phone call from Sally Mathews (Mrs. MacDonald). She is living along now with four children, ages 14, 13, 10 and 8.

Claims she can't "go" it alone - wants someone to come and see her.

Worker: O.W. Girdlestone:lg
Date: October 10, 1972.

ADDED NOTE

August 25, 1972

The situation begins with Sally Mathews (McDonald) calling me because she remembered me. Felt she couldn't manage on her present income of $1.65 an hour.....could I help?

It was about two weeks before I was able to see her in her lunch break. We had coffee in a nearby restaurant. She is quite attractive, well-kept and has tremendous drive and determination. Her situation is simply that she works as an assistant butcher at the I.G.A., but is being exploited by being only paid $1.65 an hour. In very simple terms, she just doesn't have enough money.

We discussed alternatives and she is determined not to go on Welfare or Mother's Allowance but feels that she should be allowed to work but receive sufficient income to support her children.

Retraining was discussed or perhaps further training; also hospital insurance; all the things that make life different for her.

On my return, I made three phone calls.......

(1) Mr. Groulx, Social Family Services - he agreed to send a worker to see if they could assist with a supplementary allowance.

(2) O.H.S.I.P. Office, who agreed to send Sally Matthews the application forms for coverage on a reduced premium.

(3) Canada Manpower. Mr. Verne Marks agreed to give Sally Mathews an appointment to discuss training at an adult training centre for butchering, where family accomodation would be provided, such as Elliot Lake.

October 6, 1972 - I phoned Sally Mathews to-day at work.

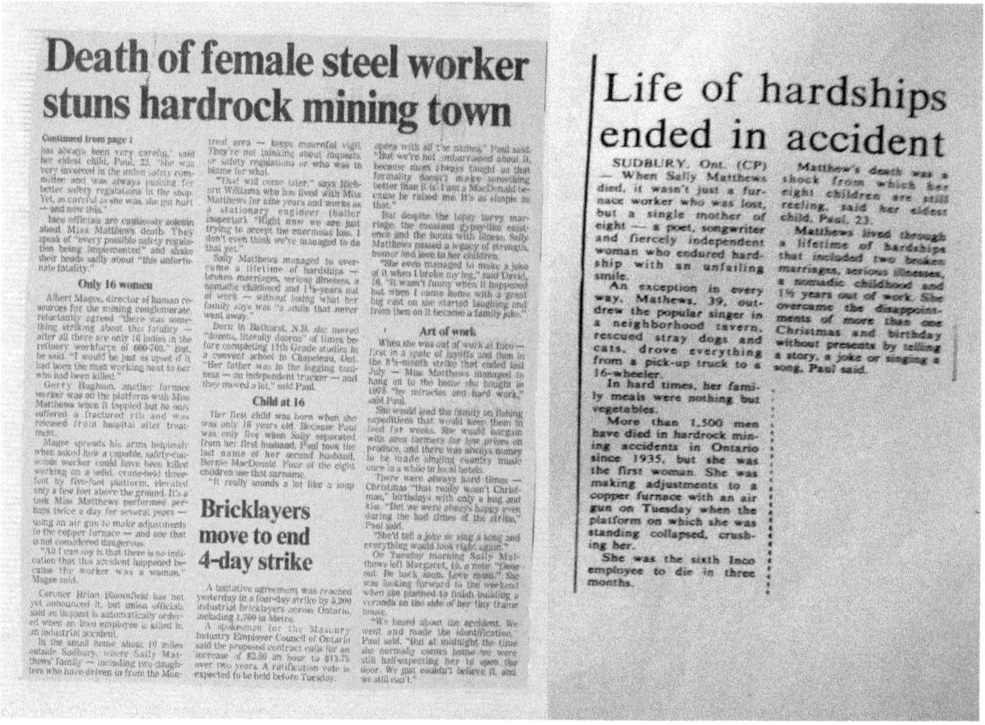

Death of female steel worker stuns hardrock mining town

Continued from page 1

has always been very careful," said her eldest child, Paul, 23. "She was very involved in the union safety committee and was always pushing for better safety regulations in the shop. Yet, as careful as she was, she got hurt — and now this."

Inco officials are cautiously solemn about Miss Matthews death. They speak of "every possible safety regulation being implemented" and shake their heads sadly about "this unfortunate fatality."

Only 16 women

Albert Magee, director of human resources for the mining conglomerate reluctantly agreed "there was something striking about this fatality — after all there are only 16 ladies in the refinery workforce of 600-700." But, he said, "I would be just as upset if it had been the man working next to her who had been killed."

Gerry Hughson, another furnace worker was on the platform with Miss Matthews when it toppled but he only suffered a fractured rib and was released from hospital after treatment.

Magee spreads his arms helplessly when asked how a capable, safety-conscious worker could have been killed working on a solid, crane-held three-foot by five-foot platform, elevated only a few feet above the ground. It's a task Miss Matthews performed perhaps twice a day for several years — using an air gun to make adjustments to the copper furnace — and one that is not considered dangerous.

"All I can say is that there is no indication that this accident happened because the worker was a woman," Magee said.

Coroner Brian Bloomfield has not yet announced it, but union officials said an inquest is automatically ordered when an Inco employee is killed in an industrial accident.

In the small house about 10 miles outside Sudbury, where Sally Matthews' family — including two daughters who have driven in from the Montreal area — keeps mournful vigil. They're not thinking about inquests or safety regulations or who was to blame for what.

"That will come later," says Richard Williams who has lived with Miss Matthews for nine years and works as a stationary engineer (boiler inspector). "Right now we are just trying to accept the enormous loss. I don't even think we've managed to do that yet."

Sally Matthews managed to overcome a lifetime of hardships — broken marriages, serious illnesses, a nomadic childhood and 1½-years out of work — without losing what her family says was "a smile that never went away."

Born in Bathurst, N.B. she moved "dozens, literally dozens" of times before completing 11th Grade studies in a convent school in Chapleau, Ont. "Her father was in the logging business — an independent trucker — and they moved a lot," said Paul.

Child at 16

Her first child was born when she was only 16 years old. Because Paul was only five when Sally separated from her first husband, Paul took the last name of her second husband, Bernie MacDonald. Four of the eight children use that surname.

"It really sounds a lot like a soap opera with all the names," Paul said. "But we're not embarrassed about it, because mom always taught us that formality doesn't make something better than it is. I am a MacDonald because he raised me. It's as simple as that."

But despite the topsy turvy marriage, the constant gypsy-like existence and the bouts with illness, Sally Matthews passed a legacy of strength, humor and love to her children.

"She even managed to make a joke of it when I broke my leg," said David, 14. "It wasn't funny when it happened but when I came home with a great big cast on she started laughing and from then on it became a family joke."

Art of work

When she was out of work at Inco — first in a spate of layoffs and then in the 8½-month strike that ended last July — Miss Matthews managed to hang on to the home she bought in 1978 "by miracles and hard work," said Paul.

She would lead the family on fishing expeditions that would keep them in food for weeks. She would bargain with area farmers for low prices on produce, and there was always money to be made singing country music once in a while in local hotels.

There were always hard times — Christmas "that really wasn't Christmas," birthdays with only a hug and kiss. "But we were always happy even during the bad times of the strike," Paul said.

"She'd tell a joke or sing a song and everything would look right again."

On Tuesday morning Sally Matthews left Margaret, 15, a note: "Gone out. Be back soon. Love mom." She was looking forward to the weekend when she planned to finish building a veranda on the side of her tiny frame house.

"We heard about the accident. We went and made the identification," Paul said. "But at midnight the time she normally comes home we were still half-expecting her to open the door. We just couldn't believe it, and we still can't."

Bricklayers move to end 4-day strike

A tentative agreement was reached yesterday in a four-day strike by 3,200 industrial bricklayers across Ontario, including 1,700 in Metro.

A spokesman for the Masonry Industry Employer Council of Ontario said the proposed contract calls for an increase of $2.50 an hour to $13.75 over two years. A ratification vote is expected to be held before Tuesday.

Life of hardships ended in accident

SUDBURY, Ont. (CP) — When Sally Matthews died, it wasn't just a furnace worker who was lost, but a single mother of eight — a poet, songwriter and fiercely independent woman who endured hardship with an unfailing smile.

An exception in every way, Mathews, 39, outdrew the popular singer in a neighborhood tavern, rescued stray dogs and cats, drove everything from a pick-up truck to a 16-wheeler.

In hard times, her family meals were nothing but vegetables.

More than 1,500 men have died in hardrock mining accidents in Ontario since 1935, but she was the first woman. She was making adjustments to a copper furnace with an air gun on Tuesday when the platform on which she was standing collapsed, crushing her.

She was the sixth Inco employee to die in three months.

Matthew's death was a shock from which her eight children are still reeling, said her eldest child, Paul, 23.

Matthews lived through a lifetime of hardships that included two broken marriages, serious illnesses, a nomadic childhood and 1½ years out of work. She overcame the disappointments of more than one Christmas and birthday without presents by telling a story, a joke or singing a song, Paul said.

ANNE-LAPPA/Sudbury Star

Anne-Marie Courtemanche endured years of sexual abuse at the hands of her stepfather, Bernard MacDonald, who was sentenced to five years in prison for the offences.

Sexual abuse victim relives horror at trial

Former Lively resident tells her story, hoping it will help others who have been victims of sexual abuse

By TERRY PENDER
The Star staff

On this particular morning, Anne-Marie Courtemanche doesn't want to be here. The man who so kindly abused her for eight years when she was a child is going to be sentenced, and she doesn't want to hear it.

"Courtemanche has her brother, John and sister Jackie with her. The three of them are looking their way through the prison halls of the Sudbury Courthouse to Courtroom A, a small room on the second floor.

"I think if people talked about this abuse more it would be less hidden," she says.

As they enter the small courtroom, the trio quickly see their former stepfather, 68-year-old Bernard MacDonald of Lively, who is sitting a few metres away on the front-row bench. MacDonald was convicted this past November of having sexual intercourse with a girl less than 14, and of ...

SUDBURY/ONTARIO

Sexual abuse victim fights back

Continued from Page A1

She doesn't remember anything else happening until she was nine. By that time, Courtemanche shared a bedroom with four of her sisters. They each had their own bed.

At night, MacDonald would come into the room and perform oral sex on Courtemanche. These assaults took place regularly, she says. Not long after this, MacDonald tried to rape his stepdaughter.

Courtemanche says that by the time she was 11, MacDonald was forcing sexual intercourse on her every week.

MacDonald and Courtemanche's mother eventually had three children together. That brought to eight the number of children living in the house. Courtemanche was too scared to say anything about the abuse.

Courtemanche's sister, Laura Landry, also says she was sexually abused by MacDonald. He would come into the girls' room, and perform oral sex on her as well. She was scared that he was about to begin raping her, but didn't want to say anything about it.

Instead, she told her mother what MacDonald was doing to her sister. The mother called the police. Courtemanche was 11-years-old.

"I remember sitting in the back of a police car, talking to the cops," says Courtemanche. "I denied everything . . . I was scared of him.

"He was beating our mother right in front of us. What do you expect?" adds sister Jackie.

According to an old file from the Children's Aid Society, the police did investigate, and Courtemanche's mother had assault charges laid against MacDonald. The file also notes that MacDonald was accused of sexually abusing Courtemanche and her sister Laura.

But nothing happened, and today it's not clear why.

"We followed the paper trail, but it just went cold," says assistant-crown attorney Susan Stothart, who prosecuted MacDonald.

The abuse continued after the police investigation. Sally Matthews soon had enough and left MacDonald in 1972. She took all of her daughters with her — except Courtemanche.

"She sent me to play baseball. When I came back she was gone with the other girls and left me at home with the boys," she recalls.

The abuse escalated and occurred much more frequently. In early 1973, when she was 15, Courtemanche was getting sick in the mornings. She didn't know why. "Bernie told me I was pregnant, and laughed about it," she recalls.

Soon after, Courtemanche learned her mother and sisters were living in Creighton. She ran away from MacDonald and joined them. Courtemanche was sent to a "home for unwed mothers" in

---

JOHN E. LIGHTFOOT JR./Sudbury Star

John Courtemanche supported his sister Anne-Marie throughout her lengthy court battle after she charged her stepfather Bernard MacDonald with sexual assault. MacDonald was convicted for the offences that occurred over a number of years when Anne-Marie was a child.

Kitchener to have the baby. The infant was given to the Children's Aid Society for adoption.

To this day Courtemanche is at a loss to explain why her mother had left her with MacDonald. For years, Courtemanche couldn't think or talk about it. It's something she was never able to resolve with her mother, who was killed in an industrial accident at Inco's Copper Cliff smelter in 1980.

"For years I felt guilty about Anne-Marie being left behind. We'll never know for sure why our mother did that. We've got to remember she was a victim too. She was beaten by him for years. She was probably scared that he would come after her, so maybe she left Anne-Marie behind to placate him," says Landry in a telephone interview from Gold River, B.C.

* * *

Defence lawyer Ted Conroy rises in the courtroom to address Judge John Poupore at MacDonald's sentencing hearing. MacDonald now suffers from phlebitis in his right leg, high blood pressure, a deteriorated disc in his back, asthma and bronchitis, and he has to take 17 different pills a day, says Conroy.

"There's been no evidence of bad conduct since that time," Conroy tells the courtroom. "You ought not to punish conduct that occurred 25 years ago as if it occurred today."

He suggests that his client be sentenced to less than two years and ordered to perform community services.

He also notes that MacDonald has put in 50 years of productive work, has raised several children, had his wife in court with him every day, and some neighbors came to court to support him as well. Clearly, Conroy tells the courtroom, MacDonald has the necessary resources to re-integrate back into the

---

community.

But Stothart wastes no time in reminding the judge that the court is dealing with a man convicted of sexually assaulting a child.

"The accused sexually abused his stepdaughter for eight years — consistently for six years. At age seven, oral sex and digital penetration, at age nine attempting sexual intercourse by placing the victim over a workbench, at age 11 sexual intercourse on a regular basis, at 15 fellatio," says Stothart.

These are "some of the most serious forms of sexual abuse that can be perpetrated on a child," she says of MacDonald's actions. "Long-term, highly intrusive sexual abuse by a stepfather, coupled with violence in the home and threats."

Judge Poupore needs only five minutes to deliberate on a sentence. As he announces it, Courtemanche sobs quietly as she holds the hands of her brother John and sister Jackie.

"Having regard to all the circumstances in this case," intones Judge Poupore, "the nature of the offences, the repeated acts, the intimidation by the offender, the breach of trust by the offender, the lack of remorse and responsibility shown by the offender, the lasting harm to the victim, and society's need to deter this conduct, this court sentences Bernard MacDonald to five years on count number one, and three years on count number two."

The sentences are to be served concurrently — or at the same time. MacDonald will be eligible for day parole after serving one-sixth of his sentence.

* * *

Minutes after hearing the judge send her former stepfather to prison, Courtemanche is smoking a cigarette, drinking coffee, and trying to integrate everything

---

that's happened.

"If I'd known that I was strong enough to go through a trial and face him again I would have done it a long time ago," she says. "I'm still scared of him even though he's going to jail. When I was younger, I thought the day would never come when I could face him on my own," she adds.

"I started feeling guilty again after the judge sentenced him," says Courtemanche. "I had to say to myself 'I didn't do anything. He did it to himself.' "

Courtemanche wants to talk about what happened to her. For years she has kept it all inside as the memories of abuse rose in her mind like a toxic vapor, often poisoning her life.

"It's a good feeling that it's all finished. I feel light, like I'm floating. It's the weight off my shoulders. It's out. I don't have it inside me anymore . . . the guilt."

Courtemanche has always felt as though she were running from something. She moved to Montreal, where she still lives, a few years after giving up the baby. She married at 19, had three children and divorced her husband after 12 years. "No matter where I went, I was alone in my little world because there were always things I couldn't talk about," she says.

"It does affect you, every day. Sometimes, even when you are making love with your husband, you have to stop, just stop. It's not a flashback or anything. You just feel so dirty."

When her marriage ended in 1991, Courtemanche saw a therapist. She started talking about the abuse and laid charges in the spring of that year.

"I don't care who knows. It's not me. It's not my fault. I think that's why a lot of people don't talk about it. They put the blame on themselves," says Courtemanche. "I'm a survivor. I'm not the victim anymore."

These are a few letters and notes The Children's Aid Society of District of Sudbury gave to Laura and me, while going through our preliminary hearing. This shows you how we fell through the cracks of Youth Protection. No one took responsibility or came forward to help us. Here is the proof. It shows you what kind of woman my mother was—sad to say not a very protective mother.

Worker: O. Girdlestone/gg

File: 13674

NAME: *McDonald*
MARITAL STATUS: *Common–law union*
MAN'S NAME: *Bernard McDonald*

<u>WOMAN's LEGAL NAME</u>: *Courtemanche} Mrs. Hector*
CHILDREN: 8
<u>ADDRESS</u>: *Niemi Rd.- near Lively, Ontario. Lively turn-off*
half a mile and then turn left. Niemi Rd. travel approximately two miles.
House is a basement.

<u>SITUATION</u>: *This case was referred to us February 241966 by a Mrs.*
McAndrew from Lifeline and the referral stated that the children were
neglected. Mother sleeps most of the day and the children take care of themselves
the best they can. Also, there is a drinking problem in the home.

<u>*March and April 1966*</u>

I went to visit with the McDonalds who live in a basement home, which they
have purchased through the local credit union. Mr. McDonald is of medium
height, weighing approximately 200 lbs and on my first visit was quite hostile
and belligerent towards me. He spoke frequently about Children's Aid in rather
bitter terms using the name "Floyd" on several occasions. I believe this was
a previous worker. Mr. McDonald works for Inco. He apparently is a steady
worker and on top of this he also drives a school bus for the local Township
from which he derives an extra income to support this large family of eight chil-
dren. His shift at the mine is a steady graveyard shift for which he receives an
extra increment.

Mrs. McDonald is of medium height but rather fair complexion and briefly
her own situation is as follows: She was and still is legally married to Hector
Courtemanche. She herself was raised in New Brunswick and her family moved
to Sarnia when she was about age twelve and she went as far as grade 11 in
school. At which time she left school to get married to Hector Courtemanche in
Sarnia in 1956.

The marriage was unsuccessful although there were a number of children
from this union. He was unable to support this family and seemed to drift from
job to job until they finally separated.

It seems that Mrs. McDonald was left with five children in the Espanola
area and lived for some time on welfare from Mrs. Arbour, welfare administra-
tor in Espanola at the time. Along came Mr. McDonald and they began living

common-law and have done since and of course there were more children from this union.

So far there is nothing to substantiate the remarks made by Mrs. McAndrew from Life Line. However, there seem to be two or three specific problems to be dealt with in the family. 1) Mr. McDonald is rather bitter about the previous experience with the Children's Aid and it becomes necessary to pacify him to the extent where we'll receive his co-operation. 2) He seems to resent somewhat the fact that he has been stuck, as he calls it, with these five children and cannot understand why there is no system by which these children could be supported to some extent. 3) Both Mrs. Courtemanche and Mr. McDonald seem anxious to do something about planning for these children, e.g.; either divorce proceedings or custody of the children in some way.

As we all know there is always more than one way of telling a story.

Chapter nineteen

Laura Dorosh, Pastoral Center Receptionist

"Some people will always throw stones in your path. It depends on you what you make of them, wall or Bridge? Remember you are the architect of your life" – Evan Carmichael.

A Letter to Anne-Marie

My dearest Anne-Marie,

I have been feeling sadness from deep inside, not enough to bring tears, and I don't quite know why. But, I am sad. Sad at the way our lives went and also sad at the loss of trust in each other. When I look back you probably pulled away in early adolescence. We were so close and you shut down, choosing not to play or interact much anymore with me. It was probably around the time I told Mom, and the police questioned us. You might have felt betrayed by me. I was only trying to put an end to the nightmare.

I forgive you for turning away from me, for not trusting me. I wanted someone to know. I wanted someone to save us. Another time another place, maybe for us it was not meant to be.

Forgive me for leaving with Mom. A guilt I live with every day. I could not make her take you and I could not ask to be left behind. I can't imagine your shock, when you returned from play to see we were gone, your pain. The pain of life was real, the fear too great for me. Forgive me.

You have a strength I don't have. You are brave beyond belief. If I were you, would I be so destroyed?

Life/death, there would have been no option for me. Death would have been my choice. I pray I never remember anything like what you endured. I am too weak, but proud to face such betrayal of power. I cry for the child in you who suffered with such awareness. I am lucky, yes. Your poor soul! How you survived. I admire your strength. Hallelujah a broken Hallelujah. I forgive you for leaving me and forgive me for leaving you. I want only peace for you and me. We are forever joined by the invisible ropes that bind us. Kindred Spirits that journey together. I love you, my sister and my friend.

Laura

Laura's Letter to Father Delaney

The day I told Mom that Dad (Bernie) was abusing Anne-Marie (leaving out his visits to my bed), she loaded the gun and buried it on top of the dresser. Dad was sleeping upstairs. Mom phoned you and you came over immediately. Anne-Marie and I thought it would be dealt with, then and there. Especially, since we put so much faith in God. Did you know you represented God in our eyes? We watched through the window of the basement as Dad came to the table. We couldn't hear what was being said. All three of you were sitting close together. Bernie's head was shaking no. You all spoke for perhaps one half-hour. You got up and left the table. On walking out you never looked at us standing there. We stood close enough. You knew we were there. You chose not to acknowledge us. You went into your car still avoiding looking at us and drove off. We knew in our hearts Bernie had denied everything and we were left to survive on our own. There was nothing to be said. You abandoned us, thus God abandoned us in that very visit. The pain went deep and the fear even deeper. If God couldn't help me, who could?

At that moment hope for anything different was abandoned. Even Mom gave up on us, choosing to believe him and never spoke of it again. Now, more than ever despair was palpable. Fear was multiplied and speaking out was shut down.

My Inner Child (Laura)

I wanted Mom to help, and I wanted her to even kill him. When she called the priest, I thought good would win over evil. But, that is not what happened. God gave up on me at that moment. Hope was gone and a new depth of fear entered my heart. I lost a lot of respect for religion and God. I was so little and so alone. I was in disbelief. Fear took on a new meaning. If evil wins, what does the future have in store? The two people who could help believed in evil over innocence.

Life took on a new level of evil. I really was alone. The devil was winning and I was so afraid. Part of me still wanted to hold on to God and a big part of me felt abandoned. So much power and faith were put into one human being, "the priest." Did you know it was true and choose not to deal with it? At this moment in writing I remember being told by Mom that the priest asked Bernie to go for counseling and to stop. So, he did believe, but no follow up. No looking at us. It all added to the same thing. "You are alone."

I suppose you are human Father Delaney, but I have a hard time forgiving you. You are held to a higher standard. May God deal with the damage you left behind with your choices! No, I don't forgive you. I do not forgive you. I leave you with a just God. Good Luck Asshole.

Letter to Social Services from Laura

What a joke! You must have just worked for the paycheck, because protecting children seemed farthest from your mind. Take a few notes and accept everything at face value. Was psychology even required? How many children had to remain in abusive lives, because you didn't know what to do with us or what questions to ask?

Even when the evidence and words were spoken you chose to turn a blind eye. No help for us. Survive on your own was the message. Nothing was ever bad enough to remove us. I lost faith in you when I was incredibly young. I have no respect for you. You were just putting in your nine to five. If there are issues, just note them and file them. Do like the neighbours and turn a blind eye.

Not sure why you existed, but it wasn't for me. You would drop in and not even speak to me. But, trust what the adults said. Did it not cross your mind they were covering their own asses?

I do forgive you seeing you were in the infant stages of growth back in the late 1960s. Protecting women and children was a new concept. I pray with the passing of time that things have changed and I'd like to believe that in today's world you'd step in and save me from the pain of our existence.

Letter to Victim Compensation from Laura

In January I applied to Victim's Compensation. I find it necessary to let you know where I am at. Please bear with me while I walk through parts of the abuse.

Back in 1991 I brought charges against my stepfather Bernard Mac Donald for the abuses of my childhood. After learning that my sister Anne-Marie Courtemanche had done so and knowing that I certainly had reason to do the same, I pressed mental, physical and sexual abuse charges against Mr. Mac Donald. When the courts in Sudbury received these charges they initially had planned for my sister and I to have our court dates separate and our charges separate. Then, of course it being the nature of a crown attorney's position the crown changed and it was decided that our charges and the court cases would be merged. From that moment on I felt alienated.

My memory is fragmented and a lot of my childhood I only plain don't remember. I have a memory of being sexually assaulted by my stepfather, and in recalling that incident, I woke up with him under my blankets, pulling off my panties and proceeding to perform oral sex on me. I knew and still know that it was him who did this to me. But, as my body went into shock and ice flowed through my veins there came a point where I have blocked any further memory into the incident and even directly after. I still felt that even though I don't remember how long it lasted, or even if he did anything more that night, I had reason to charge him and for once in my life be recognized as his victim.

For many years when I would think of what had happened that night, I was telling myself it was humanly impossible that something like that could happen. I was about six years old when this happened, although I have always remembered most of the oral sex experience I just kept telling myself it was impossible.

Many nights after this incident my stepfather tried to get at me under my covers, but I would wrap myself so tightly in my blankets—literally rolling myself into the blanket—then lay so solidly still and stiff when he came to tug my blankets off that eventually he would give up only to return another night. I would at times sleep down the back of the mattress, so the bed looked empty and other nights I'd even sleep under the bed. I don't remember if he ever managed to get at me again.

He was determined that he was going to have sexual intercourse with me. There were times when he would ask me to let him teach me my sex education. When, I would respond, "No!" He said to me on a few occasions

"Just ask your sister how much fun it is," gesturing towards Anne-Marie. He seemed to always be making and taking the opportunity to squeeze my breasts, as I was developing and grabbing at my vagina in passing. His mind was always on my sexual body. I was terrified of him and what he was capable of. His violent temper was so unpredictable and it was obvious he had no use for the children my mother had before he started living with her. Many nights I would cry myself to sleep hearing him yelling at my mother about her being "such a fucking bitch with her bunch of useless bastards." His anger always led to physical violence of some type. Either directed at my mother or at the children she had before he met her. Of course, I was one of those bastards.

I was sorry I was ever born. Life was a living hell. If I tried to please it wasn't good enough and God help me if I did something wrong, or he though I did something wrong. I remember going to school many days with stinging welts across my back and sometimes even behind my legs. Of course I would have them covered and I would never outwardly show the pain of the stinging. When he belted he was a wild man out of control and full of anger welling up from his soul. He was merciless. I remember the belt marks and when I speak of it, I still feel the sting, but I don't remember the beating itself, my mind has blocked it. I remember witnessing others being beaten, but I have blocked my own, much like the sexual abuse.

We girls were afraid of him and knew his mind was always on sexual perversion that at night we were afraid to go to the washroom for a piss for fear he might wake up and think about coming into our room. There were many nights I would just piss in my bed and now that the court case is over and my sisters and I can finally talk about the abuse I find out that there were times that they even came into my bed and pissed then returned to their own. I thought all these years I had a bedwetting problem. That's an example of the fear we lived with.

The beatings against my mother were so frequent that we could eat while it was going on, but at the same time feel sick and shake with fear, but stay silent, listening to the cry of my mother and stuffing that food down. After all, we couldn't give the impression that anything was abnormal—not even to ourselves and we were sitting in the midst of it, in denial.

One of the most terrifying moments was around the supper table. Around the supper table was a time when things seemed too unpredictable. Either he would want to talk to us, or we all had to be quiet, or something was wrong, or someone was eating wrong, or someone was looking at him, or *all fucking hell broke loose* and the whole table would be flipped over. Shaking and trembling and not knowing whether to cry or not, we would pick up things and continue like that incident didn't even happen. Well on this one night, I don't remember how it started, but my memory kicks in when I look up from my plate to hear him yelling threats at my mother and at this point he had the ivory-handled carving knife pressed into her skin on her wrist. He was holding her hand down and I could see the fear and the silent tears falling from her face. I began to shake and cry. Like most of my childhood I was aware of the others around me, but at the same time I wasn't. He yelled out, "If those fucking kids don't stop crying, I'm going to cut it off." *I stopped dead.* Holding my fear, shaking and those famous silent tears falling into my plate! He didn't cut off her hand, but what he did was show his power. When he released her, she ran and he threw the knife at her as she ran out of the house. He turned to us, slammed his fists on the table and said, "I am God!" so, loudly it shook my bones. Then he flipped the table. These are some examples of the atmosphere I grew up in.

Concerning the mental abuse, I was told there are no such charges. OK. The physical abuse was considered not as important as the sexual. It's not OK, but OK. We were left with the sexual abuse. My sister Anne- Marie remembered much more on the sexual abuse, so the case was built around her. What about me? I asked myself, but I told myself I was selfish. I spent five years going through the legal system. Watching the lawyers and even the police officer in charge of our case and giving Anne-Marie that little extra bit of support and at times hearing comments about the charges and the case that seemed to leave me on the outside! I felt I was complaining about nothing. Anne-Marie had all they needed, but the little I had would strengthen the case. I felt insignificant and petty. But, I kept coming back. I had to see this through, because maybe I just see myself as insignificant, but what happened to me was not.

On December 21st, 1995, the judge brought in the verdict. Yes, Bernard Mac Donald was found guilty on counts 1, 2, 3, but acquitted on count 4. Count 4 was my charge. My God! I *am* insignificant! My stepfather gets to be consoled with the fact that he was acquitted on my charge. I could not identify my stepfather, because although I know it was him under the blanket, I did not see his face. I have no memory of when the incident ended, so again I didn't see him leave. He didn't speak to me to indicate it was him. But damn it, it was him! I am a victim of my own mind.

Yes he was found guilty on my sister's charges, *but that is her.* Where am I? Am I his victim or not? She got to write a victim's impact statement, I didn't. The reporter wanted to talk to her, but not me. The prison phones her to keep her informed and not me. I warrant nothing. I still cry out with my silent tears—I am his victim, aren't I?

I feel so insignificant that I have a hard time convincing myself I have a right to anything you have to offer.

For more details, please read the actual copy of my statement given to the police, which I sent with my application.

Synopsis of My Eleven Years with my Stepfather Bernie (by Laura)

I was two and a half when you came into our lives. Someone who would step into a family of three toddler girls, one boy and a pregnant mother after their father abandoned them would seem somewhat of a hero. But, no one knows what happens behind closed doors. There was no support system in place in the early 1960s to help single mothers. When you arrived with groceries in hand, that was all it took. Jackie and I were hospitalized with malnutrition.

You resented all five of us, so I don't know why you stuck around. You eventually convinced Mom to give up the two youngest, Jackie and John, to social services for adoption. That year Mom got pregnant with your first child and she threatened to give it up unless she got her two children back. So soon we were six children and Mom was twenty-one years old. You were eleven years older than her.

One of my first memories was going to Mom's room in the middle of the night to probably crawl into bed with her and you were standing at the bedroom door. You said, "Get back to your bed." I never tried that again. Just the tone of your voice was threatening.

I remember many spankings in those early years. Kids gathered around pants yanked down, thrown over your knees and the belt. We all had to watch and learn. Not sure of the heinous crimes going on at our young ages, but we all had our turn in the spotlight.

We were always in trouble for something and when you drank, we were in trouble for just existing. You hated us. You called us bastards even though I was too young to know what a bastard was. Mom was at all times a bitch, a cunt.

You were always looking for reasons to slap anyone of us, including Mom. Mom was withdrawn and didn't speak much. Something as simple as having the same supper twice in a week would earn her few slaps and a kick.

Over time, slaps, straps and kicks escalated to full blown beatings. Before long Mom was pregnant again, I tried to avoid being around you, as much as I could, but that was nearly impossible living in a small house. Wintertime you'd tell us to get outside, which was fine, but we didn't have proper footwear, mittens, or hats. We would dig holes and build forts out of necessity and fun. To keep my hands warm, I'd once in a while pull them through my sleeves and park them like ice-cubes in my armpits. At times, this was very painful.

When I got back in the house I'd run my hands under hot water, which was very painful. Keep your feet moving or your toes would painfully freeze. We were forced out for hours at a time. Didn't mind it so much except for the cold!

When I was five years old I was chasing a squirrel around the yard. I hopped up on a log and jumped down the other side. I didn't fall, but my arm was instantly in agony.

Holding my elbow and walking in the house crying, I had to pass between you and some guy drinking with you. As I passed you kicked me and I almost lost my footing. You barked, "You excuse me when you go between two people."

With tears in my eyes and in excruciating pain I turned and said, "Excuse me." I'm not sure how seriously anyone took my pain. I was in agony until the next day when Mom brought me to see a doctor. My elbow was dislocated. It took one person to hold me down while the doctor popped it back into place. Very painful!

I don't know at what age you started coming into the girl's room at night. It just seemed to be something you did. I remember seeing you crawl into different beds and I closed my eyes and fell asleep.

I remember starting school and sticking to myself. Although we had a lot of kids at home, I wasn't used to interacting with other children.

I remember meeting a girl named Beverly and she got off the bus when I did. I watched where she went. We lived just up the hill from her. I remember crawling on the rock/hill behind her house and just watching her play in her backyard. I guess I was a six-year-old stalker. Eventually, we met and became friends. I never talked about the goings on at my house, but was interested in having a friend. I didn't go to her house, but her mother always had cookies for us. One ray of sunshine in my world of confusion!

Not long after, we moved. This was commonplace for our family. This was our eighth move in my short life, but we now lived on acreage. Housing was indeed quite far apart. We lived in the basement, which Bernie built. There was no insulation, just an oil stove to heat the place. The floor was cement. It was very cold at night.

Your inappropriate touching started with our spanking. Our pants pulled down your hand hitting us until you escalated to the belt. From a belt to full-out beatings where you were holding my arm and swinging the belt wildly with your other hand. My trying to move and avoid the constant out-of-control strikes and receiving welts and bloody ridges wherever the belt struck! These beatings made it hard to walk and harder to sit. Sometimes I would cry out only because I knew you wanted to hear suffering before you would consider stopping.

It got to the point where I would give the show you wanted and in the end the laugh was on you, because I didn't let it hurt as much as it could have. It was kind of mind over matter. I can feel the welts and see the spotted bloody edges if I think too much about it. The pain and stinging of the strike! The worst area was the back of the legs. Get my back, get my behind, but the back of the legs was a pain almost beyond my threshold. You would pull our ears and drag us around. Slap us on the back of the head. "Kick us in the arse" as you would put it. When you drank which was during any time off the violence escalated. No one was safe from your wrath except your three children: Mary, David and Margaret.

The rest of us little bastards needed to know our place and understand we were "good for nothing" and would never amount to anything. We needed to understand Mom was a fat bitch. I can't even count how many times you beat up Mom. Hearing her cry and being helpless wasn't the worst of it. The worst was when you expected us to accept what was happening and continue eating while you punched and kicked Mom.

For the most part we didn't talk around the table and God forbid you would get angry (which was a condition no one could control). The table would flip and you'd have to move quickly to avoid contact with everything flying and crashing to the floor. Our dishes were thick hard plastic and would do any commercial endurance test proud. Keep your head down, pick up your table paraphernalia and sit back at the table like nothing had happened. Don't make eye contact. Keep your head down—continue eating.

The most traumatizing experience around the kitchen table was when I was about eight years old. I wasn't paying attention to your belligerent yelling and when I looked up, you had Mom's hand and wrist bent over the edge of the table with a hunting knife pressed against her wrist. I don't remember much about what set you off, but I began to cry like most of the other kids and Mom had tears running down her face. You turned to us and said, "If those fucking kids don't stop crying, I'll cut the fucking thing off!" We immediately inhaled the fear and tears. My body shook and my breathing and inner terror and tears were stifled as best I could. I gasped for air between my labored breathing. When an opportunity opened, Mom ran from the table headed for the door and you reacted by throwing the knife at her, as she made a quick exit. You proceeded to stand and pound your fists on the table and proclaim, "I am God!" I have no recollection of how that even ended.

This would not be the first or last time you chased her out of the house. Not too long after this, again at the table, you struck Mom in the neck and she immediately grabbed her neck and started running for the door. I ran after her. She couldn't catch her breath as we headed down the gravel road in our bare feet. She was gasping for air. I thought she would pass out and die. When we returned later that night, the door was nailed shut with six-inch nails. We entered through one of the windows and went to bed to wake up the next morning like nothing had happened.

You loved to exercise your power over us and we thought of you as a dangerous and scary power indeed. I thought our lives hung in the balance of your happiness. As the years passed and I started developing, you would take any opportunity to squeeze my developing breasts, (which hurt like hell) or grab my crotch in passing. I was not off limits.

OK, right now I am realizing I've avoided a major event. I must return to being six years old. I don't want to go there, but I have to tell everyone. I am embarrassed and ashamed.

When I was six I woke up to you under my covers. You were pulling off my underwear. Then you proceeded to put my feet together and bent my knees up and outwards. You started to perform oral sex on me. My blood ran cold as ice. My eyes caught sight of the bare light bulb on the ceiling and I went away. I don't know when this event ended or when I returned.

But this would not be an isolated event. So many times, I had vaginal infections and was swollen red and raw. It was painful to walk. I would wet toilet paper and place it on my vagina to cool and soothe the pain. I do remember you doing this one other time and to my surprise, I started to have an orgasm and at that point I left my body. Any event after that, I don't remember. I just recalled slamming back into my body. It felt like I hit the bed at such speed my body jerked. Leaving my body was not scary. I have no recollection of being anywhere in particular. I just wasn't present to the happenings in my bed. As time went on, I tried to deter you by sleeping under my bed, or down the back wall behind the mattress. Another invention of mine was to wrap myself in my blanket. Holding the blanket out I'd wrap it around my body then lie in bed with the ends under me. When you came to my bed you struggled and struggled to get me out of the blanket, but eventually you would give up thinking I was asleep. You never spoke a word.

I was so afraid to get up at night. I had accidents in my bed (bedwetting) until I was eleven years old. The problem was, to get the bathroom, I had to pass your bedroom and the floor squeaked. I was afraid you might wake up and head into the girl's room again.

One night I remember hearing these strange sounds from the living room. I was almost too afraid to see what was happening. Mom had started work as a butcher at the IGA store. The day before this she'd cut the tip of her finger off and was taking pain medications. When I entered the living room, Mom was sitting on the lazy boy with a small table light on. She was almost unconscious and had labored breathing. I ran to her. "Mom, are you okay?" I was totally freaked out. Mom said she was having a reaction to the medication and I needed to wake up Dad. Did she know what she was asking? Asking me to approach his bed in the middle of the night?

I went to the door and could see that he did not have PJs on. I returned to Mom, who was in awfully bad shape. "I can't do it Mom. I am afraid."

She said, "Wake him; I am in need, please."

I slowly entered the bedroom saying in a low voice, "Dad, Dad."

"What?" he barked.

"Mom needs you; she's in the living room."

This got you all pissed off, but you put a housecoat on and came into the living room. "What the hell is wrong with you?"

Mom was gasping for air. She had a labored speech. She asked that you call the doctor. It was a wintry, stormy night. Once you got the doctor on the phone it was obvious the doctor was asking questions. You were getting more and more frustrated and you threw the phone onto Mom's lap. "I have no goddamn idea! Ask her!" you shouted.

I took the receiver and held it to Mom's ear. She couldn't say too much—she was going downhill quickly. She told me the doctor was coming and I hung up the phone.

How that doctor found us was a miracle let alone coming to our house in a storm? When she arrived she had my help to get Mom into her bed. You never moved a hand to help. You sat in the kitchen at the table drinking coffee. Before the doctor left she said Mom's heart had almost stopped from having a reaction to the painkillers. If we had waited much longer it would have stopped. You were just pissed to have been awakened in the middle of the night. You weren't even interested in what the doctor was saying.

The beating especially of Mom continued and your fists of anger at the table never stopped. One time, when Mom was at work, we all had just finished lunch and you told all the kids to go outside, while I cleaned up and did dishes and Anne-Marie helped you in the basement. When you finished instructing us, I wasn't impressed that I had to do all the dishes and clean up alone. I heard a voice complaining, followed by, "Yeah, we all know how Anne-Marie helps you in the basement." I wanted to look around to see who had just signed their death warrant. But the shock of it all just hit me. It was me.

You were furious and the kids scattered. I looked at you for a moment and there was fury and death in your eyes. I started to run and you were steps behind me. I ran through the kitchen. At every turn I could feel your hands just missing grabbing the clothes on my back. On the second run around, I managed to gain a few steps on you, get into my bedroom, slam the door and lock it in one quick swoop.

You slammed your fist on the door demanding I open it. I said no and backed myself up against the far wall prepared for the door to come crashing down. "You can rot in there!" you yelled.

I was shaking and crying and confused as to how and why I'd done what I did. I had at least five hours to sweat about it until Mom got home and we had supper. At supper time I was called out of my room. The fear within me did not want me to open the door. But I did and took my place at the end of the table directly across from you. I was trembling and you said something to me and I urinated right there out of sheer fear. That moment was not only terrifying, but humiliating and you used it to humiliate me in the future.

Again I have skipped over important, but frightening experiences, so I've backed up my writing even more.

You had a friend of yours over one evening and as usual you were drinking and so was, he. Somehow the conversation changed to us girls and you and Mister Locke were talking about buying and selling one of us.

You asked for one thousand dollars for Anne-Marie. I was horrified and scared to death that you thought you owned us and could even sell us. The transaction never happened, but the experience scared me and brought my fears to a whole new level. Anne-Marie and I went into our room and cried. Our beings were not safe and we had no say.

Already for years when you were drunk and sharing stupid and intimidating stories, one of us would end up being your captive audience. Sometimes everyone would be gone, but me. I'd be listening, but not really listening, making head gestures at the appropriate time to show how interesting you were (*not*). When I was in a position like this or even at times when we were all around and I just happened to be close enough, if my attention strayed you brought me quickly back with the tip of your cigarette on my skin. I yanked my burnt hand arm away and tried to be a little more alert. Cigarettes burn, hot spoons from your hot coffee and tips of red-hot matches; it didn't matter. This was your game to exercise your power.

I loved it when you had a two-day run as a truck driver. I would be free to sleep and explore the outside world. Mom slept most of the time or watched TV or read books. She did not want to be bothered by us.

There was a time when J.B., our older cousin had come to stay with us, while he started a new job at the mines. He came from southern Ontario. One night, again at the table you got angry and started slapping and punching Mom. You dragged her into her bedroom and we could hear her crying for mercy. We heard the slapping and punching while we sat at the table. J.B. had just come in and we kids were sitting around the table stuffing our meal down trying not to pay any attention to what was happening in our parent's room. It was a regular occurrence and the behavior we portrayed was expected from us. J.B. asked. "Where are your parents?"

We said, "Dad is beating up Mom in the bedroom."

J.B. got furious and as he entered the hallway towards their room he punched the wall and put a hole through it. This just escalated the terror and uncertainty of what was normal. He opened the door to their bedroom and said, *"What the hell are you doing?"*

You (Bernie) yelled, "Get the fuck out of here!"

J.B. said, "I was taught never to hit a woman." And the two of them got into a fist fight, which spilled into the hallway. J.B. had you pinned down.

It was a winter evening and Mom called out to us, "Grab your things! We are leaving!"

I remember having to step over and to the side of you and J.B. fighting. I believed one of you would not come out of it alive. I grabbed God only knows what and I ran outside. The only car we had was the Volkswagen beetle. We could not all fit in and we were not all outside. I don't even remember who drove the car that one mile to the motel at the end of our road. We were some in the car and some running down the road. Next thing, we heard gunshots. It was you shooting in the dark, towards anyone running and hitting the snow-banks. I don't remember much of J.B. after that incident. He moved on.

Once we were all at the motel, Mom called the police and reported you for sexual abuse on Anne-Marie and me. I hoped that our nightmare was almost over. How often had I spoken with Mom about leaving? The kids felt she'd listen to me, so I tried many times to talk her into leaving. She never responded, but she never told me to shut up.

Anne-Marie was the first to sit in the back seat of the police car and I was the second. As I sat in the car, Mom and the police officer were talking and I knew that they were saying that Anne-Marie had denied everything. I told them everything I was aware of about what had been happening with Anne-Marie, but I did not admit to anything happening to me. Shame and embarrassment got the best of me.

It was great staying at the motel. We could sleep in peace and eat in peace and even though we were just all sitting on beds and floor to eat, it all seemed too good to be true. It was the greatest. When we were outside walking, we were always aware that this was the motel that you had to pass to get to the house and when we saw a vehicle, we thought it might be you approaching from afar, we'd quickly hide anywhere, sometimes in ditches and along grass, until you passed.

Bliss did not last long. Within weeks Mom dropped the charges. You had to put a lock on the girl's bedroom door and we were heading back to hell house. So much for the lock, it was a lock with a hole on the outside that could be opened with a nail and you were back on the prowl in our room that very first night. In hindsight, I wonder how much mom was aware of, but just rolled over and fell asleep, leaving us prey to a monster she couldn't face.

On one occasion, you and Mom were headed to a local bar. You couldn't get a babysitter, so you had us all lined up in a row. One of us at a time you'd ask, "So what are you going to do while we are gone?" We were lined up according to age, so I was the third. We were answering things like, "Watch the door so no one leaves," or "Clean the table." Stupid things that we weren't sure were the answer you wanted to hear. With each response you back handed the person, sending them to the floor. I stood stoic and gave some sort of response, I don't remember and the next thing I knew I got the back hand and cried, crawling away on the floor. And so it went.

Now, I found myself developing and this was drawing all kinds of attention from you. You verbally asked if you could teach me sex education. Every time, I said, "No, I learn that at school."

You'd say, "Ask your sister (gesturing at Anne-Marie). It's lots of fun."

I was just disgusted at you. I kept wrapping myself up in bed sleeping under, or in the back of the mattress.

Finally, the day came when Mom planned her exit. She made sure you were on a long trip out of town. Before we knew what was happening, Mom sent Anne-Marie to play with her friend Arlene, who lived about one mile away. Once she was gone, Mom asked the rest of us girls to pack our things and get in the car. She didn't have to tell me twice, but "What about Anne-Marie?" She never answered me.

The boys were in shock at being left behind. David, the youngest, was seven and crying, "I want to come, Mom." As we drove away she never looked back, nor did she shed a tear. I did look and it was a sad and pitiful sight.

Those first few weeks were lived in fear for our lives. We still attended the same school and Anne- Marie and the boys had instructions not to speak to us. They were afraid for their lives. I tried talking to John and he couldn't get away fast enough. He turned to me, spit in my face and told me to leave him alone.

I have always felt guilt over the boys and Anne-Marie being left behind, because I was the one bugging Mom to leave.

***

This is not The End for us. We have been given a second chance at life. A life that was meant for us before it was stolen away. A life which is happier and more meaningful! We did not only survive, we also became each other's support system throughout our lives. We saw each other through years of continuous healing and supported each other through our years of navigating the court system. We've remained dear sisters through tough marriages, sick kids and life. But most of all, we are kindred spirits and best friends.

We pray somehow, somewhere that our personal experiences will awaken you emotionally. Brick by brick you too can tear down your emotional walls and begin a new life towards healing and freedom. Baby steps! Find that light at the end of the tunnel! Stay focused! The light will continue to get brighter and brighter, one day at a time, as you continue to grow. As the saying goes it always seems impossible until it's done!

Laura and Anne-Marie

Early Reaction to, *Where Are You Mom?*

"And that's why people don't come out. There's just a huge tendency within society to deny that people we admire could be capable of actually doing bad things.

While reading the book written by Anne-Marie Courtemanche titled, *Where Are You, Mom?* I had no illusions about family. The book teaches that life doesn't pretend. Family is who treats you like family. Ninety percent of the life-changing advice I've gotten came from people unrelated by blood, but connected by a sense of what family really is. Family is love as Anne-Marie has shown us in her book. It is deeper than obligation. It is looking at a person and genuinely wanting for him or her you want for yourself. There are no mirror tricks or tired clichés. This book shows that love is pure without the need of any filters.

This book helps me realize why that abusive father was put in my path, why my neglectful mom was responsible for my well-being, why that self-conscious, loathing supervisor enters my timecard, why that jealous friend continues to call and why a myriad of obstacles presents themselves in my journey. I realized they were never put there to win. They cannot be allowed to win. Misery has no idea what winning is because it is locked into what emotion losing brings.

The obstacles Anne-Marie encountered had one purpose despite their claims and that was to sharpen her, to provide the necessary pressure to bring forth the diamond residing within her. So, she can face the day with her head raised, determined. Her stepfather was an obstacle confronting her. He was a block in the road, but he was not at the end of the road. Get past that block and do what diamonds do…Shine.

With age comes wisdom. But, if you are doing the same shit year after year, I'm sorry, but you are just getting old. There is nothing wise about having the same arguments, keeping the same fake ass friends and taking the same abuse. That is called insanity.

This book leaves me with valuable advice that has had the most powerful impact on me. It has taught me that the most powerful impact on life comes from people ignored by society, street folk, elderly, ex-cons, and the homeless. It has taught me to never look down on anyone because you never know what your guardian angel is going to look like. Don't judge, listen.

I will no longer base my decisions on past hurts. I will live in the moment and not in memories that keep me afraid. Today I burnt the blanket which hid my heart and housed my fear. I will allow every new experience to wear its own diamonds and not the shackles of a past it has no knowledge of. I will never allow what has scared me to remain sacred, but rather I will move forward into what makes me smile. Old rooms and old thoughts will not interact with the dance and fragrance of my sanctuary. I will look closely into the new face and stop attempting to find similarities with the old. Everything shall be new because I am working for a better today. Tomorrow doesn't need me, today does.

Penned with love,
-Hann Monty

We lived with a hush-hush type of mentality—problems stay at home—that's just how we grew up. We never spoke about what our parents yelled at us about. Not even the simple things.

-Nadine Ratchet

Hey Sharon,
Thanks for giving me a sneak preview so I can get a feel of the book. This book is deep, I must say. As I said before we lived in a hush-hush society.

Many people out there tried to give the impression that they had it all together. Doing stupid shit; in the attempt to appear independent and grown. But, little do they know, it is not the parties, the drugs, the sex, the late nights and the alcohol that makes you a verified adult…that is called escapism. We see Anne-Marie's mother there, but she wasn't really there. Where was she? She was hiding behind an image that no one could see. Real adults don't hide. They do real, meaningful things and try to grow daily as individuals. They don't sweat the small stuff. As for the stepfather, I see so much insecurity. He had a big mouth, yes, but he was the biggest pretender in the book. I wish the social worker or even the priest had had the guts to tell him wake the fuck up!

Kudos to Anne-Marie for learning from everyone and speaking for herself; It is amazing what can be done by one who will not be handcuffed by doubt. At first the surprise overwhelmed me. I could not believe her mother turned a blind eye to what was really going on. It made me wonder, did she sell Anne-Marie to this man? But sooner, rather than later I realized that every so-called secret vanishes in a phenomenon called a positive mindset. And Anne-Marie possesses that.

Do you know; what the ironic part is Sharon? I laugh as I write that sentence, but it is not funny at all. The ironic thing about life is the so-called good people (religious, family,) taught me to judge, hate and lie. The so-called bad people (homeless, ex-cons, prostitutes) taught me to love.

I am a living witness that angels may not always have wings, but they always have compassion. My heroes always look a little different than the norm. They don't appear on magazine covers or on big-screen TVs. They don't always wear uniforms or stand behind microphones. Instead, they look like Gram holding the fort down, teaching and feeling pain when confronted with the suffering of another. My heroes always seem to care.

And as Anne-Marie exposes her soul she frees herself to become more than expected. More than the mediocre world that threatens to distract then consume her.

Make every day count for something Anne-Marie. Evolve. Drop the baggage of hurt, regret, doubt and powerlessness where you are and dare to be a shining star today and for the rest of your life. The cemeteries are already filled with corpses who never forgave themselves and spent lifetimes having regrets.

Your friend in words and deed,
Nadine Ratchet.

It's about time people come out of their shells...#Me Too movement?

She was hailed as the Queen of Pornography, but she dreamed of a handsome man who will save her from this nightmare of a life.

She still clings to her dignity but the strain of this forbidden love has become too much.

How much further can she run from public disgrace?

When will her broken heart heal?

Perhaps by telling her story she might discover a true partner, a lasting love.

Her main goal is to help others become free from this tangled web of lust, a sense of hopelessness and lies.

Anne-Marie and Sharon found each other and they dare to hope that their dream will come true, but there is one big problem.

Can they escape those who would rather see them dead than broadcast their dirty, evil secret?

How can something so wrong feel so right?

In '*Where Are You, Mom?*' Love was condemned before it begAn.

He fell for someone; he knew he shouldn't.

He made no effort to try to fight his feelings.

Each passing day he fell deeper as her lips got fuller.

Her mother hid it in every possible way.

She didn't even care.

This sex crazed man excavated the forbidden fruit.

He never thought of the horror, shame or despair.

He dug deep into her crevices and licked the gushing juice.

His soul pleasure!
While she had to learn to like it!

How will she ever be able to invite another man into her heart and ask
him to stay the night?
~Hayden Dorival

I have learned a lot from your autobiography. I am convinced there will always be male chauvinistic pigs. There are too many girls who suffer from these so-called men. I am hoping that your autobiography encourages other women to speak up against the ills of society. Clearly Bernard knew what he was doing. He was taking advantage of your mother and her situation. He didn't even pretend to care! To him females were objects. He wasn't sexually deprived, he was obsessed! And then he used fear and manipulation to feed his ego. You'd think that the gynecologist would have done more to save you from this tragedy.

I might tell you my story in another book, but here is part of the situation that changed my life. Since this incident whenever something bothered me or I could not understand what was happening to me, I took to pen and paper and I wrote on the subject that was belittling my confidence or attacking my joy. Just like Anne-Marie I too was approached by my stepfather after Mom separated from Dad when I was eight and I blocked men from my mind. I knew no man would take the place of my dear father. Dad had taught me valuable life lessons and I will cherish our memories together forever. Little did this man know he had messed with the wrong child? I wasn't about to become his next victim. So, when he wasn't expecting it, I mustered all the strength from my ancestors and I elbowed him in the testicles and then I made a dash for it before he realized he'd eaten his own words, "It won't hurt." I never wanted to feel his touches nor saw him nurse his pain. Straight to my aunt's yard I ran all the way, to tell them what the rapist tried to do to me while my mother was in the hospital having his child. I knew men were fucked up, but do they always have to prove it? Fortunately for me, with the help of my community this rascal was chased out of the village. Rocks flew like kites after him as the men from my village chased the son of a gun back to his village. It was this story that inspired me to start writing *Touch*.

~Sharon

Oh yes, there's a lot of fucked up men out there. Thank God your dad taught you to defend yourself. I'm so grateful you nailed him before he could do any harm. I wonder if these guys think since we're young we'll forget. I really don't know—they have fuck-all in their brains. Proud of you girl"

~Anne-Marie Courtemanche

Anne-Marie I really do not think these guys cared or even thought about our age. Some men are addicted to young blood. Any young thing that passes, they lick their lips. If you don't give it up voluntarily, they take it. They have no regard for what's to come while they are feasting. And when they are caught like Shaggy they will say, "It wasn't me."

-Sharon Dorival

And I sat there
stifling.
Not from lack of air
But, I just couldn't…
I couldn't
As I listened to her story
Interrupting our moment of intimacy
My girlfriend, in the midst of me touching her body
Kissing and caressing
Stopped me
And I sat there in the bed
Wondering if I turned her off
Changed her mood
And what I could do
To get the moment back again
Then she said…
"It's not you… it's me!"
And I wondered was she blowing off,

Where Are You Mom?

Putting things off
In the nice way that she normally does…
I've grown accustomed
to the shutouts.
Though they're unexplained!
For the most part, unexpected!
I was willing to respect her wishes.
But this time…
I asked why
And to that, she replied
"I want to tell you… but I can't"
But, I prodded and pleaded
Until she spilled the beans
That my touch reminded her of things
And she was afraid of being alone with me
In all this darkness
Because all she remembers
Is that time when she was just about fifteen
In the middle of the night
She was awakened as her bedroom door creaked open
And she felt his presence
The voiceless man!
She'll never forget the coarseness.
Or the alcohol and cigarette on his breath
His silent demands said
"Shhh… It's okay… it's just me"
As he slid his hands under the sheets and into her panty.
And she lay there frozen: -
She was afraid!
She was shocked!
That her own father could do her such
She tried to scream out
But, the words just didn't come out
They wouldn't sound
And for five minutes that felt like five hours

Anne-Marie Mac Donald Courtemanche & Sharon Dorival

He took advantage of her innocence
When he left she cried herself back to sleep
And first thing in the morning
She scrubbed herself clean
Trying to remove the stains
That he had left on her body and brain
She tried to tell, but nobody would listen
Nobody read her signs
Her silent plea for help
They just didn't see her
Mom didn't acknowledge
That her father did these things
And he would return weekly
Or maybe she knew, but just didn't care
The voiceless man returned weekly
To do the same over and over again
After a while she got so accustomed
That she didn't even feel anything
Or feel the need to say anything
So she turned cold to the situation
But she prayed and prayed to one day leave his household
So she left home after getting pregnant got a job after having a baby at
sixteen years old
Even though it meant that she had to forego college
Putting her dreams on hold
Less money to spend on the things that she wanted to do
She now had peace of mind and could sleep soundly at night
But every so often… he would call her
And speak of "unfinished business"
Show up at her work to see how she was progressing
It's like he was hiding in plain sight
Proud of his impudence and her ignorant of her feelings and affliction
And she lived in fear that he may follow her home
So she changed her routes and became this introvert
All the suffering… the pain… the distress

Where Are You Mom?

She spoke of so candidly
The details were troubling to me
And as she sat there in the bed
Telling me this
I cried more than she did
And she couldn't understand it
Why I was pouring out as much emotion as she did
But then I turned to her
And I let it out, finally
"My father did me the same fucking shit!"
~SAD

Dear Sharon and Anne-Marie,

It has been a pleasure tasting a slice of your masterpiece. Only brave souls take this path. It is hard for many, especially women, to write from their memory bank of hurts. I have tried my best to summarize mine in the poem above, written especially for your book, *Where Are You, Mom?* I asked myself the same question, "Where Are You Mom?" It is not easy. I wish you all the best. All healing is first a healing of the heart.

Sincerely,
SAD

Acknowledgments

Right off the bat, I need to shower some love on this fantastic team for the incredible amount of hard work and enthusiasm that they've put into bringing this book to fruition. Thanks especially to my scribe and coauthor, Sharon Dorival; my friend, Lisa Hennessy; and my one true love, Dave Koski.

None of this would have been possible without my decision to finally overcome and put pen to paper to make this happen. It is not an exaggeration to say that Lisa couldn't have recommended a better person to help me write my story and I am grateful every moment that I have Sharon in my corner. She is so patient, dedicated and passionate in her writing.

Much gratitude to everyone who read early, terrifying and messy drafts of this story and wrote me incredible, thoughtful feedback that made this autobiography so much better than I ever would have imagined it could be. I am grateful for the overwhelming amount of love and support that was sent my way by friends, family and acquaintances via social media and in person during this difficult year of gathering my thoughts and trying to help put this book together.

Much love to Gram and her family. The friendship and care they've shown me over the years have meant more to me than words can express.

Thanks to my children for having the patience with me for taking on yet another challenge that decreases the amount of time I can spend on them.

Big kudos; to the team at FriesenPress for helping me with the finishing touches! You are an amazing team, filled with professionalism and lots of patients, again thank you from the bottom of my heart.

With much respect to Laura with every compliment in the world, there's still not enough to express what an amazing sister I have and how blessed I am to have you in my life. It's amazing how you've always stuck by my side through thick and thin. You gave me the strength to fight for my life and never give up, when I had no worthwhile reason to continue. You are an awesome human being filled with great compassion and understanding. You couldn't be more of an amazing sister then you are. You are the best friend everyone dreams of having.

All the love in my heart goes to you for your bravery, resilience and strength this past year. Just when I thought you couldn't be more amazing, you went and proved me wrong. I'm so happy you wanted to help write this book. It tells the world that you too were sexually abused and you provided more detail about the abuses we were forced to endure. This will give the reader a feeling of the hell we went through. You've written many articles for magazines and were a writer for TV Guide in Thunder Bay and you put deep emotion into your writing. Love always, XXX.

This is for you Jackie; I pray this book will give you the opportunity to clarify any doubts and that it will answer any unanswered questions you may have from your childhood and give you the courage to move on and never look back. You need to recognize how far you've come. You are especially important to me and I want nothing for you, but the very best. You are stronger than you think. I raise my hat to you for raising your grandson since he was born. He is very blessed to have you for a mom, as is Crystal. Love always, XXX.

As for Paul, David, Mary and Margaret Mac Donald and John Courtemanche, I truly hope you are all at peace, with everything we have all been through or witnessed. I'm just so thankful we all made it out alive. It's so sad we were robbed of our family life, with our dysfunctional family, lacking love and support from both our parents. As the saying goes, it's the kids that pay for everything. Hope life is treating you good. I have never forgotten you. You all have a special place in my heart XXX.

Christine (Nancy) I must say there are a lot of family members and friends who are waiting to meet you with open arms. How I hope that day will come soon. I honestly can't wait until our separation is a thing of the past. I just want to get to know you as a friend or to at least meet once before tragedy hits, so you can decide about a relationship afterwards. I sincerely don't want to cause any trouble in any way, shape or form. I will continue to keep faith XXX.

I am eternally grateful to you, Gram. You instilled the greatest life values in me and they define who I am today. You will always have a part of my heart. You showed me what unconditional love and understanding were when you chose to take me under your wing. For me you were an angel sent from Heaven. I will cherish every precious moment we shared together, our birthdays, laughs, steam baths, visiting Cindy, playing Scrabble, mini crepes and so much more—the list goes on and on. I honestly can say you saved my sanity, my life. Without you, Sylvia Basto I don't know where I'd be today. You have my sincere blessings RIP. Love always, Annikki XXX.

Paappa, or Grumpy as we called you, I deeply appreciate you being our personal taxi driver. Sorry if I was a pain in the ass, but Gram put me up to it and it was fun. I enjoyed every moment and I'm sure you liked the attention. Seeing you be so grumpy made us laugh—you probably put on a show for us. I'm sure there were times you were fed up with Laura's, Lila's and my foolishness, but you were so patient. Thanks for always lighting the wood stove in the steam bath on our demand, even if at times you didn't want to. You taught me how to play solitary and how to dance the waltz and the polka—you were a great dancer. I'm having a laugh thinking of you and writing this RIP XXX.

Sorry Jack, for doing everything to bug you. NOT! I was always encouraged and protected by Gram, filling my pockets with peppermints and raiding the pantry and fridge. We would ask Gram and she'd always say yes or was easily persuaded. Much appreciation for the taxi rides to school when Paapaa couldn't and for being patient with me. It was awesome to reconnect in 2017 to have some laughs together.

Who raised you? The apple never falls far from the tree! You are a kind-hearted person. Your family and friends are truly blessed to have such an amazing person in their lives. Thank you for everything you do for everyone XXX.

To the bachelors; Eino, Emil Basto and M. Locke, thanks a million for respecting us girls. Eino you were awesome in loving and taking care of Puppy, your golden retriever (I believe) that had three legs. Emil, how impressed I was with you showing us the ships you built in Mickey bottles. Thanks for the stories, the tea and the patience. You've taught us that there are some great men out there. RIP XXX.

Arvo and Aili Basto, thanks for the tea parties and for teaching us how to play the countless board games. Many thanks for teaching us how to take care of the flowers and gardens. You would've been great neighbours and friends. You would've been amazing parents. RIP XXX.

Helen Koski, you have a heart of gold. Like a mother, like daughter. You touched my heart when you opened your home to me, when Dave and I stayed at your house in May 2017. It felt like old times—so many awesome memories. You are the same amazingly strong person I remember. I must tell the world that you are the queen of peanut butter and jam sandwiches. You have raised six awesome children. I was heartbroken to hear you fell ill. But, there is something in that Finish blood that never ceases to amaze me—you got this, Helen. I too need some of that Finnish blood. I'm extremely saddened to inform you that my beloved friend Helen has passed away suddenly as she lost her long battle with Colon Cancer, on February 22, 2021. She had plenty of wisdom to share and kept me grounded on so many levels. She, like many, has been waiting patiently for the completion of this book. Due to the COVID 19 pandemic and other minor corrections to the editing process, it has caused numerous delays, for the completion due date, which was August 2020. Unfortunately, Helen will never have the chance to read it. I wanted her to be proud of me. I could barely wait to hear her reaction. She was such an honest person.

I can imagine her looking down with her beautiful smile. Till we meet again Helen, I miss you already. I Love you so much, may you continue to watch and protect your beautiful family. May you now Rest In Peace. Love always Annikki XXX.

I can't imagine age in the neighbourhood. We learned my childhood without you, Lila. We couldn't afford to lose each other—we were the only girls around the same how to respect each other *and keep our friendship through those rough years.* I loved going to your place, especially through the Christmas holidays—you guys had so many toys and games. I remember when Paappa made your big wooden doll house with furniture—we would play for hours and have many tea parties with your porcelain tea set. Remember going to spy on the teenagers jumping off the high cliffs at the quarry? Or how about using a red cloth, trying to get Gram's bull in the field to charge at us? Holy cow did we run for our lives a few times. We were fearless out in the world. It's just amazing how we were unstoppable in exploring the world. They were the best times. It was awesome to meet up again for Sonia's wedding in July 2017 XXX.

My dear friend, Helga, the best memory I have of you is when your mom had you in her arms and was breastfeeding you. You were so tiny and just so beautiful. I would stop and just look at you in your mother's arms many times. I'm so thrilled to have met you in person in May 2017. The memories we can make are limitless. Thanks to you and hubby Phil for letting me stay and letting me get to know you more. I absolutely love the special connection we have. You are the greatest pet parents. I'll forever be grateful for the great pictures you've forwarded me through messenger. I've used them in my autobiography. You are such a compassionate person. You are an example to follow. Thank you XXX.

Tom, Kerry and Mike you boys were always nice to talk with and had fun playing basketball, tag, of course at Gram's place, teasing and running after your big pig outside in your yard. I also have great memories playing with your boxing ring, your table hockey game and so much more. You guys were pretty darn cool, whether you know it or not. Your whole entire family kept me sane. I truly enjoyed meeting up with you all in 2017. You all have a special place in my heart, XXX.

Dave, I'll forever be grateful to you for finding me on social media in 2013. I thought how insane it was and what were the chances of us reconnecting again. Whenever we connected it's just so funny how we can talk for hours and always have something new to say every time. It was an honour for me to have accompanied you for your gorgeous daughter Sonia and Adam's wedding in July 2017. It's something else for me to cherish forever. And what a great time I had with you preparing the wedding breakfast for your siblings. It did cross my mind wow nice it would be if we could always do this together as one. The importance and pride I felt to stand by your side and to be within you and your family again I truly felt I was in the right place and was so blessed to have you all back in my life. I was also pleased to meet your eldest son Wayne, a genuinely nice young man. It feels like every time we reconnect it's like we've never parted. I pray for the day we will reconnect for good and never have to part. Love always, XXX.

Kudos to my three amazing children Annie, Junior, Joey and their spouses, Ari, Shar and Martin; how understanding and incredibly supportive you've all been. You are my favourite support group. Thank you for trusting and believing in me. I gained my strength to fight and never give up because of you. You were my entire favorite success secret. Without you knowing you've all played such an important part in the success of my healing and writing my book. I surely wouldn't have made it without you. I can say I'm one hell of a proud mother—I wouldn't want to change a thing. I love seeing the interaction between you all, it truly touches a mother's heart, the love you have and express between each other. I'm also so blessed for my granddaughters Kelly-Ann and Amy; they have changed my life for the better. They are my world! May they forever be protected throughout their lives? Wow, it's crazy to see how loved and spoiled I am. I've been so fortunate to have you all in my life's journey. Having you by my side has added unimaginable happiness and stability to my life. There are no words that can express how grateful I am to be your Mom. Now, it's my turn to be your greatest fan. I will continue loving you unconditionally and I will always be there for you. Love forever and ever Mom XXX

Susan Stothart, our crown attorney, you were a bulldog in the courtroom. Anyone who has you for a lawyer is blessed. You were faced with having to defend our three mistrial calls, WOW and Susan you were such a fast thinker, with one foot always ahead of the other. We'll never forget how you had confidence in us, or you're coming back to inform us what the doctor had discussed on the phone call, that was definitely one of our most stressful moments. We literally jumped and cried with joy. Most of all, I want to thank you for believing in us. I'm sure you have an amazing great reputation. Thank you, many blessings XXX.

Police officer, Larry Dénommé, thanks for your positive support. You absolutely gave us the confidence to move on and never give up. Thanks for getting the disposable camera pictures developed and thank goodness they were all black! You too had faith in us, as we did in you. We will never forget the lunchtimes we had together. I want to thank you for showing us that great men do exist. Bless you XXX.

Victims/Witness Support Group at the Sudbury courthouse, you are all earth angels. Everything was much easier because of you. People must know they're never alone. I was honoured that you asked to put the poem I wrote on the bulletin board in the Sudbury Shopping Center. My sisters and I want to thank you from the bottom of our hearts for guiding, helping and encouraging us to hold our heads high and to never look down. Thank you XXX.

Sharon, I'm just very grateful to Lisa for introducing us—obviously, she was right, you're an awesome author. Writing the story of my life has been a surreal process. With all your support, encouragement and with no judgment, you have helped to give me a legacy to pass on to my family and friends. This is a dream come true. Thanks for standing by me with total confidence. My goal is for myself to continue to heal, which is a lifelong process. It just gets easier as time goes by. I find comfort in knowing this book could help other victims of abuse find their inner strength and their courage to break their silence and regain their life. Thanks for polishing up my story XXX.

FriesenPress, I couldn't have done this without your amazing editorial work. With your help I'm confident we will help others. I'm grateful for everything you've done to make this a success, again thank you.

Anne-Marie Courtemanche

Other Books by Sharon Dorival

To preview or purchase Sharon's collection of ebooks please visit http://www.amazon.com/

Obedience In a Me First World and *Poetry on the Run* are available for purchase at http://www.lulu.com/

You can also purchase *THROUGH MY EYES: Poetry of a Vivid Mind* on http://www.blurb.com/magazine

To see what's coming soon please visit www.sharondorival.com

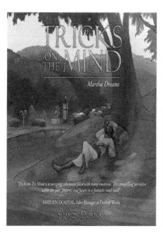 

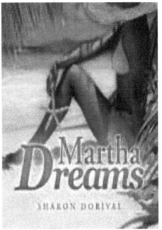

CPSIA information can be obtained
at www.ICGtesting.com
Printed in the USA
BVHW092254100422
633623BV00005B/17